vegan salads

vegan salads

OVER 100 RECIPES FOR SALADS, DRESSINGS, TOPPINGS & TWISTS

MITCHELL BEAZLEY

This material was previously published as *Nourish*

An Hachette UK Company
www.hachette.co.uk

First published in Great Britain in 2016
by Mitchell Beazley, a division of
Octopus Publishing Group Ltd
Carmelite House, 50 Victoria Embankment
London EC4Y 0DZ
www.octopusbooks.co.uk
www.octopusbooksusa.com

This edition published in 2018

Text and photography copyright
© Amber Locke 2016

Distributed in the US by Hachette Book Group
1290 Avenue of the Americas, 4th and 5th Floors,
New York, NY 10104

Distributed in Canada by Canadian Manda Group
664 Annette St., Toronto, Ontario, Canada M6S 2C8

ISBN 978-1-78472-456-6

Printed and bound in China

10 9 8 7 6 5 4 3 2 1

Publishing Director Stephanie Jackson
Art Director & Designer Yasia Williams-Leedham
Editor Pollyanna Poulter
Copy Editor Nicola Graimes
Nutritionist Angela Dowden
Production Manager Caroline Alberti
Photographer Amber Locke

CONTENTS

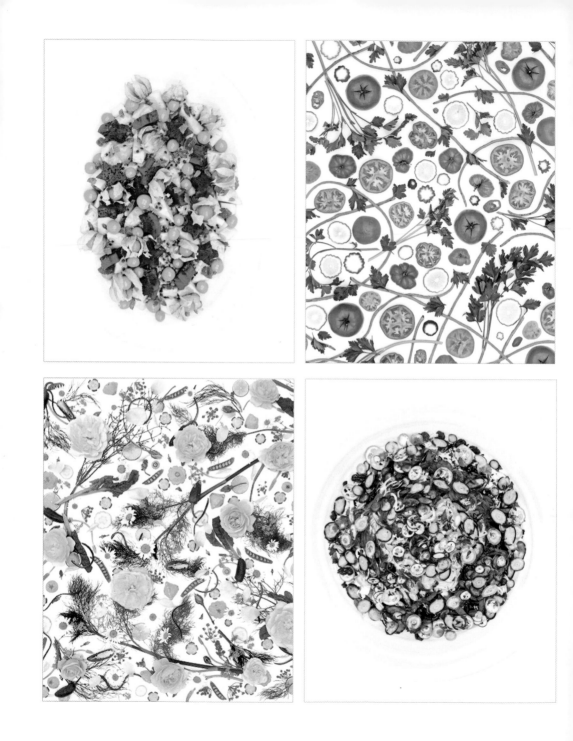

introduction

ABOUT ME

I come from a family of passionate foodies and was fortunate to grow up with enthusiastic gardeners as parents, so we always had a large vegetable patch and a bountiful supply of fruit, vegetables, salad crops, and herbs. My mother is a talented cook and bought me up to appreciate good ingredients and gave me an ingrained desire to create beautiful, nourishing food. For her, a meal needed at least seven different colors for it to constitute proper healthy eating! Unsurprisingly, salads at home were lovingly made, vivdly colorful seasonal delights, and started my passion for fresh fruit and vegetables and healthy food in general.

MY LOVE OF RAW FOOD

People choose to eat a raw food diet for all sorts of reasons but for me it was purely curiosity. I'd stumbled across the concept while reading an article in *Vogue* magazine and was really intrigued by the idea. After some research I decided to try it out for a few weeks and wow! I was absolutely blown away by how incredible it made me feel—I had a crazy amount of energy, distinctly improved mental clarity, a wonderful feeling of well-being, and I slept incredibly well too. Two years down the line, I now eat about 80 to 90 percent raw food, depending on the season, and I find this way of eating works really well for me.

I appreciate that a raw food diet might sound a bit outlandish, not particularly appetizing, or hard work, but it can be so tasty and rewarding. So if you're intrigued to try it for yourself, I recommend starting with just one raw meal a day, either a breakfast smoothie or a big raw salad for lunch or dinner. Build it up from there, and see how you feel.

When I started eating raw food it gave me a new appreciation of fresh fruit and vegetables and a fascination for creating ever-more flavorful and eye-catching salads. And after more than two years of daily salad-making, I'm still super-enthusiastic about them. For me, it's a treat at the end of the day to spend a little time in the kitchen and find different ways of creating big bowls of goodness that are not only satisfying for me and my family's appetite (we love food and like to eat a lot!), but that also taste amazing.

I love discovering new ingredients, finding new ways of preparing fruit and vegetables, and playing around with flavor and taste combinations. I'm always amazed at the infinite variety and beauty of natural ingredients, which is why I started to create designs with them.

I also get great pleasure from growing some of my own produce and I gravitate to the more unusual heritage and heirloom varieties because they have such diversity in color, taste, shape, and texture. Even if it's just picking a few fresh herbs from the garden, there's a real sense of achievement using an ingredient you've grown yourself.

ABOUT THIS BOOK

Raw salads play a major part of most raw diets, but don't think of them as just summer food or a light, unsatisfying meal made up of a few sparse, soul-less lettuce leaves. Salads can be big, bold, delicious, nutritious, and satisfying. Then there are the knock-your-socks-off dressings and toppings that will raise your bowl of wonderfulness to a whole other dimension.

This book encapsulates what I love about raw food, and salads in particular. Alongside the recipes for both sweet and savory salads, all styled and photographed by myself, you'll find a chapter on dressings and toppings as well as tips on ingredients, cutting styles, and techniques. The salad recipes comes with an explanation of their key nutrients and health benefits as well as various ideas of how to adapt them to different tastes and eating occasions. Each salad recipe serves two to four people but as a raw fruit- and vegetable-based diet is one of abundance, portion sizes are typically on the large size. Please adjust the quantities to suit your appetite and nutritional requirements.

I really hope you enjoy reading this book as much as I did creating it, and that you find my recipes and photographs both visually and gastronomically interesting.

Viva la veg!

Amber

WHAT MAKES A GOOD SALAD?

A salad can be as simple or as complex as you wish, and more elaborate preparation is by no means always better. A plate of thickly sliced sun-ripened tomatoes need nothing more than a sprinkle of sea salt, a glug of good cold-pressed extra virgin olive oil, and a scattering of basil leaves to enhance their natural perfection. For me, sometimes just a bowl of grated carrots with a basic vinaigrette hits the ultimate gustatory spot, particularly when I'm short of time.

I personally eat a HUGE salad at least once a day. More often than not I'll make it out of whatever I happen to have in the fridge, on the countertop, in the greenhouse, or in the garden. Sometimes I'll plan and shop specially and enjoy a longer and almost meditative process of chopping, grating, and slicing to create a more elaborate dish. You can even eat salad for breakfast as a blended green smoothie or juice.

People often balk at eating salads in the colder months, but if you add rich and spicy dressings (flavored with fresh ginger root, garlic, and spices, for example), include carb-dense vegetables, such as carrots, sweet potatoes, and celery root, and add extra nuts and seeds, you instantly have a more satisfying and "warming" salad. If you're a nonraw eater, then the addition of cooked vegetables, warm dressings, or sauces and hot toppings will definitely do the trick.

We sometimes think of salads being predominantly savory in flavor but adding fruits, such as strawberries, blueberries, or figs to your vegetable creations all work brilliantly. They also look lovely and give a pleasant soft texture and sweetness to your final dish.

It's always worth remembering that we eat first with the eyes, so it pays to make an effort with presentation, using good-quality fresh ingredients and incorporating a range of colors and textures.

The best way to start a salad is with fresh, preferably seasonal and organic produce for both flavor and health. If only buying organic produce, try to choose ones from the Clean 15 list and avoid the Dirty "Dozen" (see opposite). The principle is that thick-skinned fruit and vegetables absorb less pesticides than those with thin skins.

THE DIRTY "DOZEN" & CLEAN 15

Since this list first originated in 2013 kale, collard greens, and bell peppers have entered the Dirty Dozen list, making it a Dirty 14 instead*. This list, which is frequently quoted, is American in origin. While the types of chemicals and the levels of pesticides used on imported produce may differ from US produce, the principles remain the same. It is always worth choosing organic produce whenever possible.

*See the EWG Shopper's Guide to Pesticides in Produce report, www.ewg.org

DIRTY "DOZEN"

1. apples 2. peaches 3. nectarines 4. strawberries 5. grapes 6. celery 7. spinach
8. bell peppers 9. cucumbers 10. cherry tomatoes 11. snow peas 12. potatoes
13. chile peppers 14. kale/collard greens

CLEAN 15

1. avocados 2. corn 3. pineapples 4. cabbage 5. peas (frozen) 6. onions
7. asparagus 8. mangoes 9. papayas 10. kiwi 11. eggplant 12. grapefruit
13. muskmelon 14. cauliflower 15. sweet potatoes

Neutral

TOP TIPS FOR THE BEST SALADS

1. Choose a variety of fresh produce for nutritional value as well as flavor, color, texture, and esthetics.

2. Buy the freshest, high-quality produce you can. See "Tips & Tricks" on page 17 for the best ways to wash and store your salad ingredients for maximum freshness and longevity.

3. Make sure your ingredients are dry. This is so important, especially with delicate salad leaves, because a dressing won't coat a wet leaf and you want to avoid a soggy salad.

4. Try to ensure each forkful contains different elements, such as salad leaves, vegetables, fresh herbs, crunchy bits, chewy bits, juicy bits, and a hint of sweetness (from fruit or from the dressing) to give a balance of flavors and textures.

5. Some salads containing more delicate leaves are best with a fresh, light dressing, whereas others with more robust leaves and ingredients can stand up to stronger-tasting, heavier, rich or creamy dressings.

6. If you're serving your salad dressed, add it little by little to avoid swamping the ingredients. Only slaw benefits from predressing. In all other cases, add the salad dressing at the last minute (see pages 122 to 124).

7. Add some extra appeal with a few finishing touches (see toppings pages 136 to 140).

FLAVOR GRID

Ingredients can be grouped according to base flavor profiles. Using a balanced selection of these with a suitable dressing will result in interesting, highly flavored salads. As a general guide:

Neutral: most soft-leaf lettuces, cabbage, bok choy, spinach, avocado, mushrooms, cucumber

Grassy: celery, asparagus, Swiss chard, fennel, green beans, herbs

Spicy: watercress, arugula, radishes, horseradish, turnip, chiles, garlic, onions, leeks, fresh ginger root, basil, garden cress, mustard greens

Sweet: fennel, bell peppers, carrots, beets, peas, corn, sweet potato, parsnip, (ripe) tomatoes, fresh fruit and berries

Sour: citrus fruit, rhubarb, green papaya, sorrel, (less-ripe) tomatoes, lemon grass

Bitter: endive, chicory, bitter melon, kale, okra, dandelion leaves, eggplant, radicchio, puntarelle, broccoli

Bitter

Grassy

Spicy

Sour

Sweet

SALAD STYLE

If I'm making a salad just for myself I tend to gravitate toward the same favorite bowl time and time again. If I'm feeding several people, however, I love to present salads on large decorative platters. This spreads out the ingredients and there's more room to make them look attractive.

Any food looks more appealing served in a pretty bowl or on a platter. I mainly use white dishes (and occasionally black or slate gray) because I like the colors of the ingredients to really pop and stand out. I also sometimes layer a salad in a straight-sided glass bowl. If I'm taking a salad to work or on a picnic I use a big screw-top glass jar and add the ingredients in layers as I cut them up.

Salads can be presented in all sorts of ways and you can really be creative. They can be laid out like a mandala, arranged in a checkerboard pattern, or just chop all the ingredients up, throw them together in a big bowl, and mix them up with your hands.

SALAD PREP

I love the challenge of coming back from a farmers' market or grocery store and deciding exactly what to do with the produce I've bought. So in preparation of my "prep," I usually lay out the fresh produce on my kitchen table and mentally run through all the things I could do with each one and how the ingredients may work together. The variety of preparation permutations are endless (a "hundred and one ways with a carrot" anyone?) and even the most basic lettuce leaves can be chopped, torn into bite-sized pieces, shredded, grilled, braised, or used as an alternative for tacos or wraps. The challenge of making something creative and inspired with the most basic fruit and vegetables is what I sometimes have the most fun with. While there are lots of suggestions and ideas in this book, I encourage you to experiment with your own raw style.

A bed of raw vegetables and/or green leaves is always my favorite way to start making a salad and these things make the healthy base of all the salads I eat. I then add a selection of other "savory" fruit and vegetables, then maybe a few sweet or tart elements to add little bursts of flavor, and finally a sprinkle of superfood ingredients or garnishes. Sometimes I add a few cooked vegetables or some carbs or proteins, but greens and raw vegetables always make up the majority, with other elements just supplementing or adding (complementary or contrasting) flavors, textures, decorations, or extra nutritional hits to supercharge my salad bowl.

There are some vegetables, especially root vegetables, that you possibly wouldn't instantly think of eating raw, such as sweet potatoes, Jerusalem artichokes, cauliflower, broccoli stems, butternut squash, celery root, or turnips. But, sliced very thinly, they can be incredibly palatable and nutritious. If you buy organic carrots and beets, don't hesitate to use the carrot tops and beet leaves and stems. They are delicious and pack an amazing nutritional punch.

The following lists contain some pointers to the types of fresh ingredients I often use when making salads, to inspire your creativity and suggest some options:

GREENS, SUCH AS:

- **Lettuce:** Little Gem, butterhead, iceberg (often derided as bland and watery but when chilled and cut finely gives a cool crunch to a salad), Romaine, frisée, oak leaf, bok choy, Chinese leaves, corn salad
- **Radicchio:** chicory/endive, castlefranco, frisée
- **Dark leafy greens:** spinach, watercress, kale, Swiss chard, dandelion leaves (these are all extremely good for you—the darker the green color the better)
- **Cabbage family greens:** kale, Savoy cabbage, Brussels sprouts
- **Samphire, seaweed,** or other edible sea vegetables
- **Sprouting seeds and beans:** sunflower sprouts
- **Micro greens:** baby kale, pea shoots, micro-herbs
- **Beet leaves and carrot tops**
- **Handfuls of fresh chopped herbs**
- **Other lower nutrient-dense greens:** broccoli, fennel, cucumber, celery, zucchini, green beans, snow peas, sugar snap peas, fava beans

"SAVORY" RAW FRUIT & VEGETABLES, SUCH AS:

- radishes, celery, asparagus, kohlrabi, cauliflower, onion/scallions, wild garlic, mushrooms, avocado, cabbage, artichoke, okra, mooli

"SWEET" RAW FRUIT & VEGETABLES, SUCH AS:

❄ bell peppers, corn, tomatoes, carrots, sweet potatoes, butternut squash

❄ apples, papaya, peaches, apricots, grapes, figs, kiwi, clementine, pineapple, blueberries, strawberries, raspberries

❄ dried fruits, such as raisins, dates, figs

INGREDIENT SPECIFICS

ONIONS It's often nice to add an "onion-y" element to a salad, not only for an instant savoriness but, with its strong flavor, to make it seem more satisfying. Finely chopped scallions are great, as are chives and shallots, which have a much milder flavor than white onions. Red onions are sweeter and cooked onions (roasted, braised, barbecued, or caramelized) are a really nice addition, too. It's also worth quickly pickling larger onions (red or white or even shallots sometimes) before you use them. This will cut their acidity, and make them milder and more palatable to onion-haters.

I always chop onions into extremely fine micro dice or slices as thin as tracing paper using my mandoline because, unless you love raw onions, getting a big chunk can be an unpleasant experience and can overpower other flavors in the salad. Alternatively, a shake of onion salt or spoonful of onion chutney in a salad dressing is another way of working this flavor in.

GARLIC If you'd like a hint of garlic in your salad, rub a cut clove of garlic lightly around the inside of your salad bowl and it will delicately flavor your salad as you mix it. Alternatively, put a peeled clove in a jar of dressing for 30 minutes and fish it out before you serve your salad. It will give a gentle flavoring to your dressing.

CAULIFLOWER has become popular again thanks to its versatility. When roasted it takes on new flavors, while cooked and mashed it works as a low-carb replacement for traditional mashed potatoes. By baking it into a crust you can make low-carb/gluten-free pizza base. Very finely chopped or grated it takes on a plausible grainlike texture and is a perfect rice replacement. Mixed into salads it gives a pleasing texture and absorbs a dressing really well.

FIBROUS VEGETABLES that you might usually cook (like beet or squash) can be grated or sliced very finely to make them easier to digest. Sometimes it's worth marinating them, or just dressing and setting them aside for a while to soften. This works really well with things like coleslaw since the fibers of the cabbage soften so they're easier to chew. Don't overlook Jerusalem artichokes, which are really great raw. Peeled and finely sliced or grated, they add a sweet crispy crunch similar to Chinese water chestnut.

CHARRED corn, roasted bell peppers, zucchini, squash, mushrooms, and eggplant are great nonraw salad additions and give a wonderful smoky flavor. Grill halves of citrus fruit before squeezing their juice into a dressing for a beyond-delicious flavor. Next time you have your barbecue out it's worth cooking a few extra things to add to your salads during the week—it's amazing how grateful you can be later in the week for those leftover roasted vegetables with their wonderful smoky aroma.

PICKLES and fermented foods have a great sweet/sour tang. As well as being full of fantastic gut-friendly bacteria, they can really bump up the flavor—so get hold of a jar of kimchi or sauerkraut and add it to your next salad.

HERBS are a great way of adding a fresh taste and a flavor "brightness" to salads. Mint (either chopped or whole leaves) is delicious in most salads. It's fun to use a spectrum of different herbs in your salads throughout the year. Dried herbs are great in dressings, too.

Commonly used herbs include: basil, thyme, parsley, oregano, marjoram, cilantro, and chives. It's certainly worth growing some of these if you can. You can also try out some more unusual herbs, such as lemon verbena or lemon balm (especially in salads with a fruit element), marjoram, sweet cecily, lovage, summer and winter savory, the Japanese herb "shiso," or the sweet licorice-tasting "anise hyssop" (if you can get hold of some).

EDIBLE FLOWERS add visual interest, fragrance, and sometimes a subtle floral taste. Always be sure you're using blooms free from pesticides or preservatives, which means that using flowers purchased from the florist or supermarket is not a good idea. Always make sure that they are actually edible—check a reliable online resource if you're not sure.

Some of the floral, vegetable, and herb flowers I like to use include: nasturtiums, marigolds, pansies, roses, sunflowers, daisies, fuchsias, lavender, zucchini, radicchio, fava bean, sage, chive, borage, thyme, fennel, bronze fennel, dill, and purple basil.

NUTS AND SEEDS Though they are high in fat, nuts and seeds are a great addition to a salad. They add protein, fiber, and a whole host of nutrients. You can use them plain, toast and roast them, coat them in spices, or caramelize them. Leave them whole, or crumble, crush, or grate them. It's sometimes even nice to crush some and grate others, so the small gritty bits coat the salad ingredients and give a pleasant additional texture.

SALT If you're trying to reduce the level of salt in your diet then it's great to use naturally salty-tasting ingredients in your salad or dressing. Some vegetables, such as tomatoes, bok choy, celery, samphire, beets, and spinach, and herbs such as basil, have a naturally higher sodium level. Celery can be dried and ground into a great-tasting "salt" alternative, as can the stems of Swiss chard. I often use the leaves of rainbow chard for the "leafy" salad part and then very finely chop the stems so they look like confetti scattered over salads.

Left: Carrot roses take practice but prove just how stunning a plate of salad can be.

Right: Sweet & Sour Vegetable "Noodles" (see page 84).

WHY COOK CERTAIN VEGETABLES?

Cooking some types of foods decreases their nutritional content. For example, water-soluble vitamins, like vitamin C, can leach out into cooking water or be degraded by heat. Some foods have a better nutritional value when cooked. For example, the levels of lycopene in cooked tomatoes is higher and more bioavailable than in raw tomatoes. Include an element of both cooked and raw food for a balanced diet.

Some other reasons to include cooked vegetables:

- cooked fruit and vegetables often taste different than raw, especially when using different cooking methods, such as steaming, roasting, braising, baking, grilling, or broiling
- for variety and interest because they add a contrast of different flavors and textures to a meal
- some vegetables are easier to digest when cooked, especially more fibrous ones like broccoli and green beans
- they add some warmth and an element of "grounding" to a raw meal/salad (which can be especially welcome in the colder months) without the lethargic and slow-digesting heaviness that some cooked grains and legumes can give
- they add an element of quicker satisfaction/satiation but still keep a dish light and easy to digest

Try these great cooked additions in your salad bowl:

- roasted or grilled vegetables: baby carrots, bell peppers, root vegetables, squash, radishes, cauliflower, leeks
- grilled lettuce or fennel, seared slices of cucumber, smoke steamed broccoli, caramelized Brussels sprouts, thick slices of seared portobello mushrooms
- steamed or sautéed green beans, sugar snap peas, snow peas, bok choy, broccoli florets
- caramelized or broiled figs, peaches, apples, pears, rhubarb
- elements from other cooked recipes, such as mini beet burgers, garlic mushrooms, ratatouille
- some vegetables are completely indigestible raw, such as white potatoes, and so have to be cooked to be edible

Also don't ignore the value of preserved, bottled, and frozen vegetables. These can give an instant flavor or texture boost to a salad. It's always worth having a few of these on standby, just in case.

EXTRA PROTEIN OR CARBS?

To supplement a salad based on raw vegetables you can, of course, add in extra protein and/or carbs as your nutritional and dietary requirements and taste dictate.

✳ Proteins, such as nuts and seeds, tofu, and tempeh, make great vegan-friendly options and faro, quinoa, bulgur wheat, freekeh, couscous, wholewheat and corn pasta, brown and wild rice, barley, rice noodles, beans, lentils, split peas, chickpeas, mung beans, and forbidden rice (the type you just soak and eat raw) are all excellent whole-food carb choices.

✳ Extra carbs provide an easy way to bulk up a salad and are especially important if you expend a lot of energy or do a lot of exercise. Carb ingredients always soak up more dressing than vegetables, so adjust your quantity of salad dressing accordingly.

SALAD TIPS & TRICKS

A few tips and tricks to help with your salad-crafting:

GO FOR VARIETY Eat the rainbow of colors of fruit and vegetables. It is more interesting to vary what you buy and eat but you also get a lot more benefit from eating a wide range than always consuming the same—even superfood—ones.

KEEP IT AS RAW AS POSSIBLE Eat some vegetables (most, if possible) raw. Try not to overcook the rest, because heat degrades the nutrients, especially water-soluble ones, which are prone to leach into the water.

MAKE TIME Unless you're opting for a bowl of ready-prepared leaves or simply some chopped or grated vegetables, it can certainly take time to make a more elaborate salad and an extra-special dressing to go with it. I save as much time as possible by preparing things the night before (for lunchtime salads), using the grating disks on my food processor, and always keep a jar of my basic vinaigrette dressing in the fridge. However, when I have the time I enjoy the ritual of washing, chopping, blending, and mixing and cherish the opportunity to present my loved ones with a huge bowl of goodness prepared with love and care.

Left: Smashed Cucumber Salad (see page 74).

WASHING DELICATE LETTUCE LEAVES AND HERBS

If you have the time, wash your produce before you store it. This a great way to save time when you are ready to prepare your salad. For leaves that are too delicate for a salad spinner, place them in a bowl or sink of cold water, agitate the leaves with both hands to wash off any dirt, let them sit for a few minutes to allow the dirt to settle to the bottom of the bowl. Then use both hands with your fingers spread wide to fish the leaves out of the water and let as much water drain from them as possible. Place on a dish cloth covered with absorbent paper towels then gently roll up or fold into a parcel, place in a plastic food bag and put in the salad or crisper drawer in your fridge. The paper towel will continue to draw moisture from the leaves and keep the leaves fresh for 3 to 4 days.

WASHING VEGETABLES
One method of cleaning fruit and vegetables (other than just a quick scrub under running water) is soaking it in a solution of 1 tablespoon of baking soda plus 1 tablespoon of apple cider vinegar or lemon juice per 4 cups of water. Let the vegetables soak in the solution for 10 to 20 minutes, then drain and rinse well.

REVIVING WILTED VEGETABLES
More robust vegetables, like carrots, radishes, beets, celery, asparagus, Swiss chard, and flat-leaf parsley can be brought back from a softened, wrinkled state to crisp firmness by placing in a bowl of water in the fridge overnight to rehydrate. Alternatively, stand things like celery, rhubarb, and carrots upright in a large jar of water until they have revived.

STOPPING FRUIT AND VEGETABLES FROM DISCOLORING
Apples, pears, and avocado can sometimes discolor quickly and I've always dipped them in lemon juice to prevent this. However, I now just spray them with a very fine mist of water or briefly dip them into a bowl of water. The water acts as a barrier to prevent air getting to the cut surface to oxidize and discolor it.

SQUEEZING LEMONS
If you are squeezing a lemon using a reamer or traditional juicer, first roll the fruit on a hard surface, pressing gently with the palm of your hand as you do so. This breaks down some of the cell walls and makes it easier to release the juice once the fruit is cut. If you're serving lemons to squeeze at the table, cut each lemon in half diagonally, for ease of handling.

ZESTING CITRUS If you're using a citrus fruit just for its juice, zest it first (particularly if it's unwaxed and organic) and freeze the zest in a resealable food bag for future use. Citrus zest has a zingy bitterness and pleasing texture and enhances not only salad dressings but chocolate, tomato sauce, ice cream, and pastry. I personally like to run whole lemons (rind, pith, flesh, and all) through my juicer as it gives a powerful-tasting lemon "juice" to add to green juices, hot toddies, and salad dressings, or to pour over steamed greens or smoky barbecued meats.

CHOPPING HERBS If you need a larger quantity of a fresh soft-leaf herb, one of the easiest ways to achieve this (rather than painstakingly plucking all the leaves from the stems) is to hold the bunch of stems in one hand, and with a large sharp knife in the other, "shave" the leaves and tender stems from the bunch.

TRANSPORTING SALADS If you plan to take your salad any distance it's a good idea to layer it with the heaviest/wettest ingredients on the bottom and the more delicate and drier things on the top. Or, if it's a larger quantity salad, then take all the ingredients separately in plastic food bags to prevent the different elements from getting crushed. Always take the dressing separately too (small jam jars are ideal for this) and dress your salad at the last minute. If you regularly eat salads at work, keep a handy-sized bottle of dressing or balsamic in your desk drawer.

BLANCHING If you're blanching vegetables to serve in a salad, such as green beans, fava beans, or broccoli florets, then resist the temptation to "refresh" them under cold water because this waterlogs them and prevents them from soaking up a dressing. Just cook them for a slightly shorter time, drain them well, and place on dish cloths lined with paper towels and let stand somewhere cool. Once they've cooled down either dress them separately or add them to your salad.

SOAKING SEEDS To maximize the health benefits of nuts and seeds soak them first in a bowl of water, ideally overnight. Some require longer soaking than others (there are plenty of guidelines for this on the internet) but by doing so it kicks off the germination process and starts to unlock much of the stored nutrition, along with enzymes that make them easier to digest. Rinse and drain nuts and seeds well after soaking and if you want to go a stage further then try sprouting (see opposite). The soaking process makes the nuts and seeds softer and easier to digest and also easier to blend if you're making a nut- or seed-based dressing.

SPROUTING SEEDS There are some nuts, seeds, and beans that are better for sprouting than others. You can even sprout seeds in a jam jar in your backpack if you're traveling, so you're never without a boost of nutrition to add to a meal.

MAKING DATE PASTE This makes an excellent raw alternative to sugar or sugar substitutes. Place 8 pitted Medjool dates in a small bowl with just enough water to cover and let soak for 2 to 3 hours (or overnight). Remove the dates from the water and blend in a high-speed blender with a couple of tablespoons of the soaking water to form a thick paste. Thin down with more soaking water if you prefer a runnier "syrup" consistency. Store in an airtight container in the fridge for up to 2 weeks.

INFUSING VINEGARS These are really simple to make and you can use a wide variety of ingredient combinations for flavoring, such as rosemary, orange, lemon, fennel, star anise, oregano, marjoram, tarragon, shallot, fresh horseradish, garlic, thyme, and raspberry. To do this, wash and dry your flavoring ingredients well, chop up smaller if necessary, and divide between 2 x 16-ounce sterilized glass jars. Heat 4 cups of white vinegar in a large saucepan until it's just barely simmering then pour into the two jars, leaving a little space at the top. Seal with airtight lids and store in a cool dark place for 2 to 4 weeks. You can leave the flavoring ingredients in the jar as you use up the vinegar (the flavor will get stronger over time) or discard them. Keep the infused vinegar refrigerated once opened.

Alternatively, for a nonheated version, just add your flavorings to a bottle of vinegar and let stand to infuse for 10 to 12 days. The flavor will be much more subtle than the heated-vinegar method but still distinctive.

INFUSING OILS For instant flavored herb oil just place a handful of fresh herbs in the bowl of a food processor fitted with an "S" blade and pour in enough good-quality oil to cover. Blend until the herbs are finely chopped or blitzed into the oil completely. You can then use immediately or store in an airtight container in the fridge. If you want a clear oil then strain well before using or bottling.

SUPERCHARGING YOUR SALAD If you want to supercharge your salad try adding a few superfood ingredients, such as goji berries, chia seeds, or nuts and seeds. Or, you can add a superfood powder (such as spirulina, baobab, or cacao) to your dressing.

KITCHEN KIT

To make a salad you need nothing more than a sharp knife and a cutting board.

A simple box grater and a vegetable peeler are handy to have, and to make dressings a jar with a lid and a measuring spoon will suffice. However, if you fancy getting a little more creative, then with a few extra implements you can really have some fun. These are the tools I like to use:

* high-speed blender with different size jars

* super-sharp mandolines

* microplane graters with different blades for zesting and coarse grating

* whisks—a small one for everyday use and a large balloon whisk

* aerolatte (a milk frother for making foamy dressings)

* melon baller (a standard-sized one, a mini melon baller, and an oval-shaped one)

* selection of sharp knives—a large cleaver and smaller knifes for delicate work

* crinkle-cutter knife

* channel knife

* basic vegetable peeler

* julienne peeler

* vegetable pencil sharpeners (for making shavings and ruffles)

* lemon zester (for zesting lemons and decorative scoring)

* spiralizers—a standard one and one for making angel hair strands

* various cutters (cookie, pastry, and vegetable cutters, and a pasta wheel)

* food processor with grating disks, slicing disks, an "S" blade, and a citrus press

* sprouter for home-sprouted seeds and beans

* lemon juicer and reamer

* various measuring cups and spoons

CUTTING TECHNIQUES

Most fruit and vegetables are exceptionally delicious raw, and when very finely sliced (or shaved paper-thin) even the more fibrous ones become easy and palatable to eat. Using different styles of cutting and chopping adds interest and variety from a visual and textural point of view, and you can greatly enhance the appeal of a dish with just a few simple techniques.

The way you cut a fruit or vegetable can also influence its flavor in a dish. For instance, sliced very finely, some strong-tasting ingredients, such as onion or fennel, have a much less dominant taste than if they were cut into large chunks. So it's worth bearing this in mind when you prepare a salad.

gaufrette-style
zucchini

mandoline-sliced
yellow beet

ribbon-cut carrot using a
vegetable "pencil" sharpener

These are the different cutting techniques I like to use, all of which you can find in this book:

✳ **ribbon:** wide, long, fine slices using a vegetable peeler

✳ **spiralize:** thick noodles, fine noodles, angel hair noodles, or ruffles using a spiralizer

✳ **mandoline:** various thicknesses using different blades

✳ **julienne:** cut by hand or with a julienne peeler into long, thin slices

✳ **dice:** cut into small squares

✳ **chiffonade:** shredded or finely sliced—perfect for leafy greens and herbs

✳ **allumette:** short and long matchsticks

✳ **baton:** long, thin, rectangular shape

✳ **crinkle-cut:** also zig-zags (thick and thin), wavy-edged dice, or gaufrette-style waffles using a serrated wave knife

✳ **balls:** melon-ball size, mini melon balls, oval balls

✳ **cookie-cut shapes:** stars, squares, hearts

✳ **riced:** use a box grater or food processor—perfect for cauliflower or broccoli florets

✳ **shred:** cut by hand, vegetable peeler, or grater

✳ **grate:** coarse, medium, or fine

zig-zag-cut
candy cane beet

julienne-cut
zucchini

mandoline-sliced
patty pan squash

cookie-cutter-cut
carrot slices

salads
&
slaws

AVOCADO "TRUFFLE" SALAD

Avocado can be used to make savory "truffles," which look interesting in a salad or can be speared onto toothpicks to serve as a canapé. Here, I've simply scooped out the avocado flesh with a melon baller and rolled the balls in a mixture of seeds to give an extra superfood boost to the salad.

A light vinaigrette dressing, such as the Herb Vinaigrette (see page 126) or Grilled Citrus Dressing (see page 129), adds a mildly acidic balance to the richness of the avocado and will lightly coat the delicate salad leaves, rather than weigh them down.

2 large handfuls of mixed green salad leaves
3 to 4 tablespoons mixed seeds, such as sesame, hemp, and poppy seeds
2 to 3 large ripe avocados
1 small handful of sprouted seeds
Herb Vinaigrette (see page 126) or
Grilled Citrus Dressing (see page 129)
1 small handful of edible flowers, to garnish

Avocado provides healthy monounsaturated fat and vitamin E, which protects cells from damage. But take care if you're watching your waistline because they can provide quite a few calories.

Place the salad leaves in a shallow serving bowl. Put the seeds in a separate small bowl.

Cut the avocados in half and remove the seeds. Using a melon baller, scoop out balls of avocado or cut the flesh into large cubes. Roll the avocado pieces in the seeds until coated and place on top of the leaves.

Scatter the salad with the sprouted seeds and either serve immediately or cover and store in the fridge for up to a day or two. Because the avocado is coated in seeds, the flesh won't oxidize and turn brown.

Pour your dressing of choice over the salad and scatter with the edible flowers just before serving.

BOK CHOY & SAMPHIRE SALAD

Samphire (sea asparagus) is a wonderfully nutritious vegetable that grows in coastal parts of Britain and is delicious to eat raw. It's tender and succulent yet crunchy, and has a gentle salty taste. It's best to buy it as fresh as you can and if you can't get hold of any, substitute it with other edible fresh sea vegetables such as arame, sea palm, or dulse.

I've used it in this crispy mixed salad with bok choy and bell peppers and dressed it simply with lime juice and a little chopped green chile. A sweet and spicy vinaigrette would also work well, such as the Sweet & Sour Dressing (see page 84).

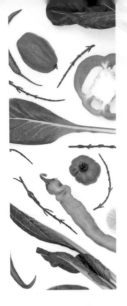

Sea vegetables, like samphire, are a very rich source of iodine—a mineral vital in the production of thyroid hormones that control metabolic rate.

14oz samphire or other edible
fresh sea vegetable, trimmed
2 large bok choy or choy sum
4 to 5 mixed bell peppers (green, red, orange, or yellow)
1 green chile
finely grated zest and juice of 3 limes

Wash the samphire well and chop the stems and leaves of the bok choy.

Seed the bell peppers and chop into small dice or slices (or a combination of the two). Seed the green chile and finely chop.

Put the samphire, bok choy, and bell peppers into a bowl or on a platter and squeeze over the lime juice before scattering with the lime zest and chopped chile.

Also try with...

Try lightly steamed or roasted asparagus, as an alternative to the samphire.

FIG & POMEGRANATE SALAD

Figs are great in a salad—they look pretty and have a gentle
sweetness and soft texture. They are also one of the truly
seasonal fruits that don't seem to be available all year round,
so are a treat to look forward to come late summer.

This salad is based on rich, deep colors with the glistening
flesh of the figs and sparkling pomegranate seeds giving it a
jewel-like quality.

2 red leaf lettuces
1 Little Gem or 4 Romaine lettuce leaves
6 to 8 large figs
$\frac{1}{4}$ to $\frac{1}{2}$ red onion, peeled
2 to 3 pomegranates

Figs are a very good
nondairy source of
bone-friendly calcium.
By weight, figs contain
more iron than steak.

Tear both types of lettuce into bite-sized pieces. Cut the figs into
quarters or thick slices and very finely slice the red onion.

To remove the seeds from the pomegranates, cut them in half. Then,
placing your hand over a large bowl, hold one half of a pomegranate
with the cut-side facing downward and bash the outside with a rolling
pin. The seeds should easily dislodge and be captured in the palm
of your hand with the juices falling into the bowl. (Wear an apron to
do this because the juices can splatter!) Repeat with the remaining
pomegranate halves.

Put all the salad ingredients in a bowl, gently toss together, then
arrange on a serving platter. Pour any pomegranate juice left behind
in the bowl evenly over the salad and serve.

Try this . . .
The figs and onions can be roasted to give this salad a new twist.
A handful of roasted or spiced nuts would be a nice addition, too.

BROCCOLI & SPROUT SALAD WITH CAPERBERRIES & OLIVES

Broccoli and Brussels sprouts are great in raw salads because their robust structure means you can shave or slice them really thinly and they still keep their texture and bite. They're also fairly bland in flavor so pair well with strong-tasting ingredients such as the scallions, capers, caperberries, and olives in this dish.

If Brussels sprouts are out of season, white or green cabbage work just as well; after all, sprouts are just like mini cabbages.

10½oz Brussels sprouts
2 to 3 scallions, trimmed
1 head of broccoli
3½oz preserved pitted green or black olives
2½oz preserved capers and/or caperberries
2 tablespoons pickling liquid from the jar of olives or capers
1 tablespoon cold-pressed extra virgin olive oil
3 tablespoons hemp seeds, or any other seeds
salt and pepper

By combining a powerful duo of cruciferous vegetables—broccoli and Brussels sprouts—this salad will bump up your intake of folate and vitamin C.

Finely slice or shave the Brussels sprouts into wafer-thin slices and chop the scallions (both the white and green parts).

Break the broccoli into florets then finely chop them in a food processor, or you could cut the florets into small pieces with a knife.

Mix the broccoli, Brussels sprouts, and scallions together in a bowl and add the olives, capers, and caperberries, chopping some before adding, if desired.

Make a quick dressing using the pickling liquid from the olives or capers and whisking it together with the olive oil and some seasoning. Pour the dressing evenly over the salad, toss well, and sprinkle with the hemp seeds before serving.

Give it some crisp . . .

The outside leaves of the Brussels sprouts are great roasted until crisp and then scattered onto the salad to add contrast to the finely shaved raw ones.

RED CABBAGE &
ZUCCHINI RUFFLE SALAD

Deep purple in color, the acai berry (normally sold in powdered form) is classed as a superfood. The powder makes a dramatic colored Acai Berry Dressing (see page 135) for this salad, or you can just sprinkle some of the powder on top, as I have done here.

I cut the zucchini into large ruffle shapes using one of the disks on my spiralizer and, if you want to keep the salad 100 percent raw, you could substitute the pomegranate molasses for date paste or a sweetener of your choice.

Acai is famed for its antho-cyanin antioxidant content and is a source of vitamin E, which scavenges free radicals in the body that can damage cells.

3 zucchini, trimmed
½ red cabbage
3 to 4 radishes, trimmed
Acai Berry Dressing (see page 135)
1 handful of mixed sprouted seeds

Using a spiralizer, cut the zucchini into ruffles or "noodles," or simply grate them using a box grater instead.

Finely slice the cabbage and the radishes and arrange all the salad ingredients on a serving platter or in a bowl.

Pour the acai berry dressing evenly over the salad. It is quite dark and sinister in color, so if you mix it into the salad you'll have a spooky-looking dish. Sprinkle with the sprouted seeds before serving.

For a cooked alternative . . .
Braise the cabbage first and add to the salad with a handful of chopped golden raisins.

RADISH, BEET & ORANGE SALAD

This is a lovely fresh-tasting salad to make in the winter months when blood oranges are in season. And if you can get hold of yellow beets as well as red, this salad is even more esthetically pleasing.

Cutting the beets, red onion, and fennel into wafer-thin slices makes them more digestible when eaten raw. If you don't like the pungency of raw onion, let it marinate in the lemony dressing for 30 minutes and its flavor will soften significantly.

3 blood oranges
2 raw red beets, scrubbed or peeled
2 raw yellow or golden beets, scrubbed or peeled
5 to 6 radishes, trimmed
¼ to ½ red onion, peeled
1 fennel bulb
1 handful of edible flowers or herbs, to garnish

LEMON DRESSING
finely grated zest and juice of 1 lemon
2 tablespoons extra virgin olive oil
salt and pepper

Fennel is a traditional stomach soother, and beets—a good source of iron, folate, and nitrates—have been shown to help lower blood pressure.

Remove the pith and skin from the oranges and slice the flesh into segments. It's a good idea to do this over a bowl to collect any juices.

Very finely slice both types of beets, the radishes, red onion, and fennel (it's great if you have a mandoline to do this, or use the slicing disk on a food processor, or cut by hand with a sharp knife). Place the vegetable slices in a large bowl with the orange segments.

To make the dressing, whisk together the lemon zest and juice with the olive oil and seasoning in a bowl. Mix in some of the orange juice, if you like.

Pour the dressing evenly over the salad and toss the ingredients gently with your hands. Transfer the salad to a serving platter and scatter with a few edible flowers or herbs.

For a cooked alternative . . .

Wrap the beets in foil and place them in a hot oven (400 to 425°F) for about 1 hour or until tender and then peel and slice when cooled. The fennel and radishes can be roasted, too. Cut the fennel into slices ½inch in thickness but leave the radishes whole. Lightly coat the vegetables in cold-pressed extra virgin olive oil, season, and roast for 25 to 30 minutes until tender. Add to the salad when cooled to room temperature.

SUMMER SQUASH SALAD

This pretty salad, made with paper-thin shavings of raw
zucchini and summer squash combined with pea shoots and
edible flowers, is pepped up with a Gremolata-style Dressing
that is rich with herbs (see page 133).

I've used yellow and green zucchini and patty pan squash but
any varieties will do, just as long as they're reasonably young,
small, and tender and not too watery.

2 to 3 zucchini, a mixture of green and yellow, trimmed
2 to 3 summer squash, such as patty pan
1 handful of pea shoots
Gremolata-style Dressing (see page 133)
1 handful of edible flowers, to garnish

Zucchini are a good
source of potassium and
folate, while pea shoots
provide high levels of
vitamin C and vitamin A.

Very thinly slice the zucchini using a mandoline or speed peeler.
Repeat with the summer squash then tip everything into a serving
bowl or onto a serving platter. Scatter with the pea shoots.

Serve the salad with the dressing poured evenly over the top, or
separately on the side. Scatter with the edible flowers to serve.

For a light meal . . .
Serve this summery salad with low-fat protein foods, such as edamame beans.
Cooling and refreshing, the salad would also make a good side dish to accompany
barbecued food.

AVOCADO, TOMATO & LETTUCE SALAD

Avocado, tomato, and lettuce work very well together in a salad, and if your avocado is really ripe you can mash it into a guacamole-type dressing.

It's best to make this when tomatoes are at the peak of their season so they're really flavorsome and need little extra help in that department other than a sprinkle of sea salt and maybe a swig of good-quality cold-pressed extra virgin olive oil.

I love using different varieties of tomatoes and here I've suggested the large Coeur de Boeuf and the tiny Tomberry.

Tomatoes are packed with lycopene, and avocados with vitamin E. Studies suggest that these two nutrients work together in reducing the cell damage that's linked with heart disease and cancer.

2 to 3 avocados
1 large butterhead lettuce
10½oz to 14oz mixed tomatoes,
such as Coeur de Boeuf and Tomberry
cold-pressed extra virgin olive oil, for drizzling
salt and pepper

Halve, peel, remove the seeds, and dice the avocados. Then tear the lettuce into bite-sized pieces.

Chop the tomatoes into chunks or cut into slices, reserving any juices that remain on the cutting board to use to dress the salad.

Combine all the ingredients in a bowl, adding the juices from the tomatoes. Season to taste and add a drizzle of olive oil.

Protein boost...
Sprinkle the salad with some hemp seeds for extra vegan protein.

WALDORF SALAD

This is a version of the summertime classic, with the
traditional mayonnaise replaced with a creamy
Raw Cashew Mayo (see page 131).

I've used red-skinned apples, here, and sliced them with
a serrated crinkle-cutter knife to give a pretty crinkled edge.

1 large handful of seedless red grapes
1 large handful of seedless white grapes
3 to 4 celery stalks, trimmed
2 red-skinned apples
1 large handful of walnut halves
Raw Cashew Mayo (see page 131)
celery leaves, fennel fronds, or dill, to garnish

Iron and omega-3 are two
nutrients that can be difficult
to get from a vegan diet,
but this salad provides good
amounts of both thanks to
the cashews and walnuts.

Pick both types of grapes from their stems and halve them. Finely
slice the celery stalks.

Core the apples and cut them into julienne strips or thin slices.

Place the grapes, celery, and apples into a large serving bowl with
the walnut halves. Add half of the raw cashew mayo and mix gently to
combine all the ingredients.

Scatter with a few celery leaves or fronds of fennel or dill. Serve the
remainder of the vegan mayonnaise on the side, or keep it
for another day.

PINK RADISH, BEET & YELLOW BELL PEPPER SALAD

This vibrant pink and yellow salad is crisp, sweet, and crunchy.
The watermelon radishes can be substituted with regular or
English Breakfast radishes, and you could use yellow or red
beets instead of the candy cane beets, if you prefer.

The pale green flecks of the Ranch Dressing with Herbs (see
page 130) look pretty with the colors of this salad, but you
could also try the Moroccan Dressing (see page 134), which
is flavored with ras-el-hanout.

2 large raw candy cane beets, scrubbed or peeled
1 large watermelon radish, trimmed
1 small yellow zucchini, trimmed
1 small green zucchini, trimmed
2 yellow or orange bell peppers
Ranch Dressing with Herbs (see page 130) or
Moroccan Dressing (see page 134)
1 small handful of mixed herbs, such as oregano,
dill, and bronze fennel fronds
1 small handful of edible flowers, such as violets,
borage, and sage flowers
salt and pepper

The beets and potassium-
packed vegetables in this salad
can help keep your blood
pressure levels healthy. Yellow
bell peppers have more than
double the vitamin C content
of oranges, so eating them
helps keep your immune
system healthy, too.

Very thinly slice the candy cane beets, watermelon radish, and
zucchini using a sharp knife or mandoline.

Core and seed the bell peppers and thinly slice into rings.

Arrange the salad ingredients on a serving platter or in a bowl
and pour over your dressing of choice. Season and scatter with
the fresh herbs and edible flowers just before serving.

CARROT, ORANGE & RED CABBAGE

Carrot and orange have a natural flavor affinity and when combined with red cabbage they make for an eye-catching color combination.

I lightly toasted the sliced almonds for the photograph so they'd stand out in the picture, but you can keep them untoasted. If you're making this dish ahead of time, don't add the almonds until the last minute.

If you're using organic carrots and they come with their green tops, wash a few fronds then finely chop and scatter them over the finished dish.

This salad supplies all of your daily vitamin A needs. Almonds add some healthy fat, as well as calcium, magnesium, and iron.

½ large red cabbage
3 to 4 large carrots (I often use a mixture of orange and purple ones), scrubbed or peeled
3 oranges
1 cup sliced almonds
1 small handful of coarsely chopped parsley or torn basil leaves

Finely slice the red cabbage and slice, grate, or cut the carrots into ribbons using a vegetable peeler. Put the vegetables in a serving bowl or onto a serving platter.

Finely grate the zest of the oranges, then cut away the peel and pith and segment the flesh, discarding the white membrane. If you do this over the bowl of vegetables, the juice will be amalgamated into the salad and act as a light dressing.

Place the orange segments in the bowl or onto the serving platter and scatter with the flaked almonds and herbs.

Protein boost . . .
Diced marinated tempeh, or a handful of cooked black beans would all add valuable protein to this salad, and taste good too.

CAULI-FLOWER SALAD

There's been something of a cauliflower revolution in recent years and the once quietly humble vegetable has been thrust into the culinary spotlight, becoming a new darling of the kitchen and many restaurant menus. The cauliflower's low-carb properties and mild taste make it an excellent, plausible replacement for rice, potatoes, and starchy grains, and there seems to be boundless love for its magical role as a pizza crust.

Thickly cut slices of cauliflower can be pan-cooked or roasted in the oven to make great "steaks" and oven-roasted, spice-dusted florets make a transformative side dish or snack. However, raw is when it really shines. Grated by hand or in a food processor, it looks like grains of "rice" and makes a great base for salads. It is quite bland in flavor, so pair it with a really punchy dressing such as the Moroccan Dressing (see page 134) or Rose Harissa Dressing (see page 129).

Here, I've used purple cauliflower and green romanesco (a cauliflower/broccoli hybrid) as I love the combination of colors. I've also added some raw okra for added crunch and a few edible flowers to decorate.

1 small cauliflower
1 small romanesco
4 to 5 okra
Moroccan Dressing (see page 134) or
Rose Harissa Dressing (see page 129)
1 handful of edible flowers, to garnish

Cauliflower is a good source of vitamin C and folate, and is also part of the cruciferous group of vegetables, which are thought to have cancer-protective properties.

Cut off the outside leaves of the cauliflower and romanesco, but keep any small tender leaves as these can be "riced" with the florets. Break into large florets and either coarsely grate or finely chop in a food processor. If using a food processor, be careful not to overprocess as the vegetables can quickly become mushy. Tip the "riced" cauliflower and romanesco into a bowl or onto a platter.

Thinly slice the okra and scatter it over the "rice." Pour your dressing of choice over the salad. Scatter with the edible flowers just before serving.

Low-carb alternative . . .
This makes a healthy substitute to regular white or brown rice.

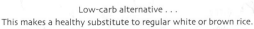

BEET CARPACCIO

I have made this salad before with dark, reddish-brown beets. Thinly sliced, red beets look remarkably similar to carpaccio made with beef or salami, but I absolutely couldn't resist using candy cane beets, here.

For the matchstick vegetables, I used sweet potatoes, pink Chinese radish, and yellow squash, but any colorful vegetables that slice easily, hold their shape, and can be eaten raw, will do.

A great dressing to serve with this would be the Sun-dried Tomato Dressing (see page 130).

A source of iron and folate, this beet salad is also a good choice if you're trying to keep your blood pressure at a healthy level.

1 large raw candy cane beet, scrubbed or peeled
2 large pink Chinese radishes or 3 to 4 regular radishes, trimmed
1 to 2 apple-sized yellow squash or yellow zucchini, trimmed
2 large sweet potatoes, peeled
cold-pressed extra virgin olive oil or Sun-dried Tomato
Dressing (see page 130)

Thinly slice the candy cane beets and chop the other vegetables into long, thin matchsticks.

Drizzle the candy cane beets with a little olive oil for a glistening effect or mix everything together with the dressing of your choice.

Try this . . .
You could also roast the vegetable matchsticks to make a bed of crispy vegetable "fries."

LITTLE GEM "TACOS"

Little Gem (or small Romaine) leaves are ideal for making "tacos." This salad has an interesting combination of flavors and textures with mild-tasting crisp lettuce, a creamy avocado and sweet red bell pepper salsa, a tang from the lime, plus a crispy topping of sprouted seeds.

If you want to take this dish to work for lunch or a picnic, the salsa can be easily transported in a screw-top jar. It can also be made in advance and stored in an airtight container in the fridge.

If your avocado is really ripe then you could mash it with the other ingredients to make a kind of guacamole. It will still taste delicious.

2 Little Gem lettuces
1 large handful of sprouted seeds (I used mooli/radish sprouts)
edible rose petals, to garnish
lime wedges, to serve

AVOCADO & RED BELL PEPPER SALSA
finely grated zest and juice of 2 limes
2 ripe avocados
1 red bell pepper
1 small handful of mild red chiles, or to taste depending
on how hot they are and your taste preference
2 scallions, trimmed
1 small handful of chopped mixed herbs,
such as parsley, mint, chives, and dill
salt and pepper

> Avocado is a great source of heart-healthy monounsaturated fat, while sprouted seeds supply antioxidants, B vitamins, and protein.

To make the salsa, pour the lime juice into a bowl. Peel and remove the seeds from the avocados and cut into small dice. Add them to the bowl and toss them in the lime juice to stop them from discoloring. Core and seed the red bell pepper and chiles and cut them both into small dice, mincing the chiles if you prefer. Finely slice the scallions. Mix all the ingredients together, including the lime zest and herbs, and season with a little salt and pepper.

Gently separate the Little Gem leaves then wash and dry them.

When you are ready to serve, fill each lettuce leaf with a spoonful of the avocado and red bell pepper salsa and scatter with a few sprouted seeds.

Arrange the filled leaves on a platter, scatter with a few fragrant rose petals for a summery look, and serve with some extra wedges of lime for squeezing.

For a protein boost . . .
Try adding small cubes of marinated tofu or tempeh.

MIDDLE EASTERN-INSPIRED SUMMER SALAD

Candy cane beets are one of my favorite summer vegetables.
I love their crazily pretty pink and white candy stripes
and sweet, mild taste. They're not as juicy as red beets, and
so are much easier to prepare raw, and their flavor reminds
me of a cross between a beet and a radish. If you can't get
hold of them, substitute radishes or red or golden
beets (raw, not cooked).

I like to serve this with the fragrant Moroccan Dressing
(see page 134) and a sprinkling of pretty rose petals.

2 crisp lettuces, such as Romaine
2 to 3 raw candy cane beets and/or raw red or golden beets,
scrubbed or peeled
1 handful of shelled pistachio kernels
1 handful of pomegranate seeds
Moroccan Dressing (see page 134)
ras-el-hanout and fresh edible rose petals, to garnish

The pistachio kernels and
pomegranate seeds give
this salad a nutrition kick
because together they're a
good source of antioxidants,
vitamins C and E, fiber,
and potassium.

Simply tear the lettuce leaves into bite-size pieces.

Slice the beets very thinly using a mandoline or vegetable peeler,
or carefully cut into wafer-thin slices with a small, sharp knife.

Coarsely chop the pistachios and then gently combine all the salad
ingredients together in a large bowl.

Pour the Moroccan dressing evenly over the salad, sprinkle with a
little ras-el-hanout, and scatter with a few fresh rose petals, to garnish.

Why not try . . .
Try the dressing poured over a couscous salad or a platter of roasted vegetables.

CRUNCHY CARROT & BEET SALAD

The Raw Cashew Mayo (see page 131) lends a rich creaminess to this salad, while the hazelnuts give it a pleasant savory crunch. I've toasted the nuts (before crushing them) so they stand out visually, but if you're keeping this salad completely raw then leave them untoasted.

Packed with all the main cell-protective antioxidant vitamins (A, C, and E), this salad also provides anemia-protective iron from the cashews.

3 to 4 Little Gem lettuces or 1 large Romaine lettuce
2 to 3 large carrots, scrubbed or peeled
1 large raw red or yellow beet, scrubbed or peeled
1¼ cups hazelnuts
½ quantity Raw Cashew Mayo (see page 131)
1 small handful of chopped mixed herbs, such as mint, basil, and parsley

Tear the lettuce leaves into bite-sized pieces and scatter on a large platter or place in a serving bowl.

Very thinly slice the carrots and beet (a mandoline is ideal for this) and crush or chop the hazelnuts.

Add the carrots and beet to the lettuce and pour over the raw mayo. Mix the salad together gently with your hands, then scatter with the hazelnuts and herbs before serving.

DANDELION, PARSLEY & BERGAMOT

Dandelion or other wild greens are packed with nutritional goodness. Be careful when you pick them to ensure they've not been exposed to car exhaust fumes or pesticides drifting over from fields nearby. Wash the leaves very well before use.

If you have room in your garden it's worth cultivating a few dandelions to add variety to salads. They're also really delicious if you grow them in the dark under an upturned plant pot so the leaves are paler and a little less bitter.

It's great to eat citrus fruit with dark leafy greens since consuming vitamin C increases your ability to absorb the iron in the greens. I've used bergamot oranges, which are typically used for their aroma (particularly in the perfume industry). If you can find them they're well worth buying, if only to experience the incredible fragrance when you cut them.

Parsley contains more than double the iron level of red meat and more than three times the vitamin C content of oranges.

2 to 3 large handfuls of dandelion leaves
or other green salad leaves
3 to 4 large bunches of flat-leaf parsley
juice from 2 bergamot oranges or regular oranges

Chop or tear the dandelion leaves into small pieces and cut the parsley leaves off of the stems.

Place the dandelion and parsley in a large bowl and squeeze the juice from the bergamot oranges evenly over them.

Bulk it up . . .
If you want to make this more substantial, add Romaine lettuce and maybe some mango or avocado.

KALE & RADISH SALAD WITH BLUEBERRY DRESSING

I've used white kale in this salad because it's so decorative. However, the normal green variety is just as good, if a little more strongly flavored. The watermelon radishes provide a decorative contrast and the vibrant purple color of the blueberry and cashew dressing adds a dramatic touch, as well as a superfood boost. The sweet and creamy dressing also counteracts the slight bitterness of the kale.

2 cups blueberries
¾ cup cashews
2 large bunches of kale
3 to 4 watermelon radishes or regular radishes, trimmed
salt and pepper

It's been shown that blueberries help to relax the walls of blood vessels, potentially reducing the risk of hardened arteries. Cashews are an excellent source of iron, so are especially good for vegans and vegetarians.

Using a high-speed blender, blend half of the blueberries with the cashews, seasoning, and ½ cup water until smooth and creamy. You may need to add a little extra water to the dressing to loosen it to a pouring consistency. Set aside until needed.

Tear the leafy parts of the kale away from the stems and chop the leaves very finely.

Thinly slice or shave the radishes and add the kale and the radishes to a serving bowl.

Pour the blueberry and cashew dressing evenly over the salad and scatter with the remaining blueberries.

Roast or juice . . .
Roast the radishes whole until tender for a nice contrast to the kale's sprightliness.
Juice and drink the kale stems, rather than throwing them away.

EDAMAME BEAN SALAD

Edamame beans are young soybeans that are picked before they start to harden so they're tender and fresh—a little like young fava beans. They're a great source of protein and are a general all-round nutritional superfood, and so are particularly beneficial in a vegan diet.

They're combined here with avocados speckled with poppy seeds and served on a bed of matchstick carrots (I've used purple, orange, and yellow carrots).

Any citrus or creamy dressing, or the spicy Rose Harissa Dressing (see page 129) would work well with this salad.

3 to 4 large carrots, scrubbed or peeled
1 to 2 ripe avocados
2 tablespoons poppy seeds
1¾ cups shelled edamame beans
dressing of choice

You've got to love edamame— these beans provide a complete source of protein, along with healthy, slow-release carbohydrate and fiber. Teamed with the vitamin-rich vegetables they make a salad that's a balanced meal in its own right.

Cut the carrots into fine matchsticks (there's no need to peel them if they are organic) using a mandoline or julienne peeler, or coarsely grate them—they'll taste just as good. Place them in a serving bowl.

Halve, peel, and remove the seeds of the avocados, then cut the flesh into large chunks. Put the avocado chunks in a bowl and lightly coat them in the poppy seeds.

Place the edamame and avocado on top of the carrots and pour the dressing of your choice evenly over the mixture.

MIXED TOMATO & HERB SALAD

This salad is lovely to make in the summer when there's an abundance of ripe tomatoes and garden herbs. I like to dress it simply with a little olive oil and a squeeze of lemon juice and seasoning.

The ingredients are all very delicate, so you can drizzle them with the simple dressing as you assemble the salad: first add a layer of chopped tomatoes to your bowl with a few green leaves, then add a drizzle of olive oil, a little squeeze of lemon or lime juice, and some seasoning, then repeat with more tomatoes, leaves, and dressing.

To make the salad more substantial and boost its nutritional content, you could add a few handfuls of chopped young kale leaves and slices of cucumber. I like to cut grooves into the skin of the cucumber to give it a pretty frilly edge when sliced.

If you prefer a more substantial dressing, then the Pistachio Pesto (see page 132) would work really well.

14oz to 1lb 2oz ripe tomatoes
7oz baby green leaf salad
1 large handful of chopped mixed herbs, such as parsley, dill, and chives
1 tablespoon cold-pressed extra virgin olive oil
1 lemon or lime
salt and pepper

This salad provides lots of healthy lycopene (from the tomatoes) and the olive oil will help this fat-soluble antioxidant to be absorbed better.

Coarsely chop the tomatoes and tear any larger salad leaves into bite-sized pieces.

Layer the tomatoes, salad leaves, and herbs in a serving bowl, drizzle with a little olive oil, and add a squeeze of lemon or lime juice between each layer as you go. Season to taste.

Veggie boost . . .
Sun-dried tomatoes and roasted bell peppers make lovely additions.

RADICCHIO & PICKLED GRAPE SALAD

I've used three different types of radicchio in this salad. The pretty, deep red colors of the rossa di Verona and spearlike leaves of the treviso contrast visually with the cream and pale-pink speckled castelfranco. The crisp, bitter leaves are tempered with a zesty orange vinaigrette and little bursts of spicy sweetness from the pickled grapes.

This salad supplies plenty of immune-enhancing vitamin C and some fiber. Bitter radicchio leaves are a good source of folate and antioxidants.

2 handfuls of small seedless black grapes
3 different kinds of radicchio, including treviso, castelfranco, and rossa di Verona
2 tablespoons cold-pressed extra virgin olive oil
salt and pepper

PICKLING LIQUID
finely grated zest and juice of 1 orange
2 tablespoons raw apple cider vinegar
1 tablespoon date paste or sweetener of your choice
2 star anise
a pinch of fennel seeds
a pinch of crushed red chile flakes
1 teaspoon salt

Place the pickling liquid ingredients (except the orange zest) in a bowl with 3 tablespoons water and stir until combined.

Stir the grapes into the pickling liquid and let stand at room temperature for 30 minutes or in the fridge overnight.

Tear the radicchio into bite-sized pieces and place in a serving bowl. Remove the grapes from the pickling liquid (reserving the liquid) and scatter them onto the leaves.

Put 2 to 3 tablespoons of the pickling liquid, the reserved orange zest, and olive oil in a bowl and whisk to combine. Season to taste, and pour the dressing evenly over the salad.

Perfect pairing . . .
Scatter with spiced caramelized nuts.

RAINBOW CHARD & BLACK RADISH SALAD

This is quite a masculine-looking salad—if there is such a thing! The strong, dark colors of the Swiss chard contrast with the bright white flesh of the black-skinned radishes (or black mooli), while the fiery kick from the Ginger & Wasabi Dressing (see page 134) make it a very "purposeful" dish.

2 bunches of Swiss chard
1 large black radish, trimmed
Ginger & Wasabi Dressing (see page 134)

Swiss chard supplies vitamin A and magnesium, a mineral that can help contribute to a reduction in tiredness and fatigue.

Tear the chard leaves away from the stems. Place the leaves on top of each other, then roll them up lengthwise into a cigar shape and cut into thin slices, chiffonade-style. Place the leaves in a bowl, separating the strands as you go.

Cut the black radish into matchsticks by first cutting it into thin disks, then stacking them on top of one another before slicing into thin sticks. Scatter the sliced chard leaves with the radish sticks.

Pour the ginger and wasabi dressing evenly over the salad just before serving.

Bulk it up . . .
A veggie burger would make a tasty addition for vegans.

MASSAGED KALE SALAD WITH ORANGES & CRANBERRIES

Massaging a dressing into the kale leaves helps break down their tough fibers until the leaves become soft and silky. The sweet orange dressing works well with the slightly bitter kale.

I've combined the kale with some finely chopped white cabbage for extra crunch and oranges and dried cranberries for sweetness. A few finely sliced fresh cranberries also add texture and a gentle tartness.

Nutrient-packed kale (rich in lutein, folate, iron, and vitamin A) teams here with proanthocyanidin-rich cranberries, which are a traditional remedy for urinary tract infections.

3 large oranges
2 to 3 tablespoons cold-pressed extra virgin olive oil
1 large bunch of kale, such as cavolo nero (dino kale)
1 cup fresh cranberries
¼ cup dried cranberries
salt and pepper

Finely grate the zest of the oranges, then cut away the peel and pith. Segment the flesh, discarding the white membrane. It's best to do this over a bowl to catch any juices. Whisk together 1 to 2 tablespoons of the orange juice in the bowl with the zest, olive oil, and some seasoning to make a dressing.

Tear the leafy parts of the kale away from the stems and remove any tough veins in the leaves. Tear the leaves into 1- to 2-inch pieces and place them in a large bowl.

Pour the orange dressing over the kale and start to massage and crush the leaves with your fingers—it will take a while for the leaves to yield but they will gradually start to soften and become more pliable and tender. The leaves are done when they feel silky soft.

Thinly slice the fresh cranberries and coarsely chop the dried cranberries and add them to the kale with the orange segments.

Let stand for 30 minutes or overnight in the fridge for the flavors to mingle and develop. Mix again before serving to distribute any juices in the bottom of the dish.

Protein boost . . .
Rich-tasting protein foods, such as toasted nuts and seeds, work well with the bitterness of the kale and the sweet and sour acidity of the oranges and cranberries.

ZUCCHINI "NOODLE"
& OLIVE SALAD

I love all the different green-on-green colors of this salad and if you're
a fan of capers and olives the incorporated dressing is a real treat.

The strong flavors of the dressing work well with the neutral-tasting
zucchini and the shower of grated cauliflower gives the visual impression
of grated Parmesan cheese, as well as a pleasant texture.

3 to 4 zucchini, trimmed
3½ to 5½oz preserved green olives
1¾oz preserved capers
finely grated zest and juice of 1 lemon
1 handful of mixed soft-leaf herbs, such as basil, dill, mint, and parsley
1 garlic clove, peeled
2 tablespoons cold-pressed extra virgin olive oil
1 large cauliflower floret

This salad provides
plenty of potassium,
folate, and some
healthy fats, too.

Cut the zucchini into long strands using a julienne peeler or spiralizer
and set aside.

Coarsely chop half the olives and half the capers by hand (remove the stones
first if the olives need pitting) and set aside.

To make the dressing, add the remaining olives and capers to the bowl of a food
processor along with the lemon juice, zest, herbs, and garlic. Keep the machine
running while trickling in the olive oil to make a chunky, salsa verde-type sauce.

Place the zucchini "noodles" in a bowl and add the dressing, mixing it in gently
with your hands. Scatter with the chopped olives and capers and grate
a snowy dredge of cauliflower evenly over the top.

Try this . . .
Try sprinkling it with nutritional yeast flakes.
The dressing makes a great pasta sauce.

FRISÉE & FIG SALAD

The sweetness of the figs and the Sharon fruit (also known as Israeli persimmon) balance out the bitterness of the frisée lettuce in this salad.

If you can, wait until your Sharon fruit ripen fully because they almost turn into a different fruit. It takes some trial and error since you have to leave them until the skins turn brown and they look as though they're about to turn rotten, but the flesh inside transforms from having a soft texture that tastes mildly sweet to an almost jellified texture with a deep caramel taste and an incredible depth of perfumed sweetness.

If they aren't fully ripe, use them as they are and moisten the salad with a dressing. The Citrus & Beet Dressing (see page 128) or Sweet Smoky Paprika Vinaigrette (see page 127) would both work well.

1 large frisée lettuce
2 large carrots (I used purple ones), scrubbed or peeled
4 ripe figs
3 Sharon fruits (Israeli persimmon)
Citrus & Beet Dressing (see page 128) or
Sweet Smoky Paprika Vinaigrette (see page 127) (optional)
¾ cup walnuts

The figs and carrots in this salad boost your intake of iron, calcium, and vitamin A. In addition, you'll get heart-healthy omega 3 fat from eating the walnuts.

Tear the frisée leaves into bite-sized pieces and slice or grate the carrots (there's no need to peel them if they're organic).

Slice the figs and chop the Sharon fruit into chunks, unless you're using particularly ripe ones. In that case, cut them in half and use a spoon to scoop out the flesh.

Combine the ingredients with your dressing of choice, if using, and scatter the salad with the walnuts to serve.

ZUCCHINI & CANDY CANE BEET SALAD

I confess I have something of an obsession with candy cane beets, as you may have noticed from their prevalence in this book. They're an old heirloom cultivar, botanically called 'Chioggia' and are much drier in texture than red beets, more like a cross between a beet and a radish. I love their crazy psychedelic pink and white stripes and they are fun to play around with in a salad. They look pretty either thinly sliced across the equator (downward gives a different effect) or sliced into matchsticks, or zig-zags as I've cut them here.

This salad goes well with the Creamy Turmeric Dressing (see page 135), but you could also try the Peanut Satay Dressing (see page 134) or the Citrus Ginger Dressing (see page 127).

3 Little Gem lettuces or 1 large Romaine lettuce
3 to 4 zucchini, trimmed ·················
2 large raw candy cane beets, scrubbed or peeled
Creamy Turmeric Dressing (see page 135)

Zucchini are a good source of potassium, which is important for maintaining healthy blood pressure.

Tear up the Little Gem or Romaine lettuce leaves and place in a bowl.

Cut the zucchini into fine strands using a julienne peeler, or grate them using the coarse side of a box grater, or you could spiralize them.

Cut the candy cane beets into matchsticks or into a zig-zag shape using a serrated crinkle-cutter knife.

Arrange the salad ingredients on a platter and pour the creamy turmeric dressing evenly over them.

Carb perfection . . .
A couple of handfuls of cooked quinoa or freekeh would boost the carbohydrate content of this salad.

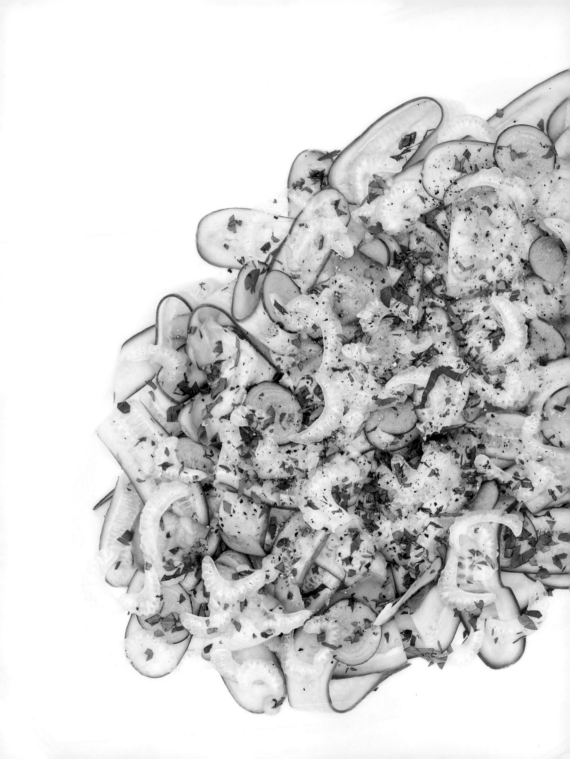

CUCUMBER "NOODLE" SALAD WITH RAW SAFFRON CREAM

These transparent, glasslike cucumber "noodles" are really refreshing served chilled in the summer with the Raw Saffron Cream, reminiscent of old-fashioned creamy salad dressing.

2 large cucumbers
3 to 4 celery stalks, trimmed
1 small raw yellow beet, scrubbed or peeled
1 small handful of chopped parsley or other soft-leaf herb
pepper

RAW SAFFRON CREAM
½ teaspoon powdered saffron
¾ cup cashews or macadamia nuts
¼ garlic clove
1 scallion (white part only)
½ to 1 teaspoon date paste or sweetener of choice
a pinch of ground paprika

The nuts in this dressing are a great source of the kind of essential fats and monounsaturates that help lower cholesterol.

Slice the cucumbers lengthwise into long, thin ribbons using a mandoline or sharp knife, and finely slice the celery and yellow beet. Place the vegetables on a serving platter or in a bowl.

To make the saffron cream, place all the ingredients and ¾ cup water in a high-speed blender and blitz to a smooth, pouring consistency. Add a little extra water to thin the dressing if needed. (If you have time, you could soak the nuts for about 8 hours, or overnight, to soften them before blending.)

Spoon the saffron cream over the salad, scatter with the parsley, and grind over some black pepper.

Perfect pairings . . .
This dainty salad is good as a refreshing addition to a Chinese or Asian-inspired meal.

SWEET POTATO & PEA SALAD

Raw sweet potatoes are a recent find for me but since I've discovered how delicious they are when thinly sliced, I now use them raw in salads all the time. They're quite dry in texture, so absorb any dressing really well. It's good to team them up with juicier ingredients, such as the peas and asparagus in this recipe, for a contrast in color, texture, and flavor.

With this salad, you could try a sweet and sour dressing, such as the Sweet Chile & Lemon Dressing (see page 130), or the Maple, Lemon & Ginger Dressing (see page 128).

4 large sweet potatoes
1 black radish or 4 to 5 regular radishes, trimmed
6 to 7 asparagus spears, woody ends trimmed·········
1¼ cups freshly podded or defrosted frozen peas
1 small handful of mixed chopped herbs, such as mint, chives, parsley, and basil
Sweet Chile & Lemon Dressing (see page 130) or Maple, Lemon & Ginger Dressing (see page 128)

Asparagus is a superb source of folate needed for cell division and blood formation. It's also a very important nutrient during pregnancy.

Scrub and wash the sweet potatoes well and peel if you don't want to eat the skin. Slice them into wafer-thin disks or grate coarsely.

Cut the black radish into matchsticks and slice the asparagus into small disks by cutting them across the stems.

Combine all the ingredients in a serving bowl with the dressing of your choice.

Try this . . .
The sweet potatoes can be cut into chips, lightly coated in coconut oil, and roasted until crisp and golden before being scattered on the salad.

SMASHED CUCUMBER SALAD

It might seem a little extreme to smash up the cucumbers, but the rough edges of the pieces soak up the Middle Eastern-style Za'atar Dressing (see page 134) really well and look unusual in this salad.

Cucumber is hydrating and very low in calories, while sesame seeds are high in anemia-protective iron.

4 large cucumbers
Za'atar Dressing (see page 134)
3 tablespoons sesame seeds
red chiles, to garnish

To smash your cucumbers, hold one firmly by the end and gently bash it with a rolling pin, being careful not to splatter the juices and pieces of cucumber everywhere. Cut any larger pieces into chunks then repeat with the rest of the cucumbers.

Place the cucumbers on a serving platter or in a bowl and pour the za'atar dressing evenly over them. This salad really benefits from marinating for 30 minutes or so. Mix again just before serving, scatter with the sesame seeds, and garnish with the red chiles.

For a cooked alternative . . .
Sear the cucumber on a hot, ridged grill pan until lightly charred in places.
The freshness of this dish would work well with any Middle Eastern-style meal.

CRUNCHY WINTER VEGETABLE SALAD

Raw winter root vegetables are so much easier to eat and digest when they're cut into wafer-thin slices. To bring out the aniseed-flavor of the fennel, serve this salad with the Tarragon Vinaigrette (see page 126), or scatter with a few fresh tarragon leaves or fronds of bronze fennel before serving.

The pumpkin seeds are delicious just as they are or you could try toasting them in a dry or lightly oiled skillet for a few minutes until they are slightly brown at the edges and have popped open slightly. They have a wonderful toasted flavor and crunch. If you salt them afterward they make a great snack, too.

2 red leaf lettuces
2 to 3 raw yellow or red beets, scrubbed or peeled
1 fennel bulb
Tarragon Vinaigrette (see page 126)
3 tablespoons pumpkin seeds
1 small handful of chopped mixed herbs, such as thyme, chives, parsley, and tarragon

Pumpkin seeds are an excellent source of zinc, which is needed for cognitive function, fertility, and reproduction.

Tear the lettuces into bite-sized pieces and scatter them over a large serving platter.

Very finely slice the beets and fennel and add them to the platter.

Pour the tarragon vinaigrette over the mixture and toss gently. Scatter with the pumpkin seeds and chopped herbs to serve.

Flavor favor . . .
Try roasting the fennel until tender to give it a milder, sweeter flavor.

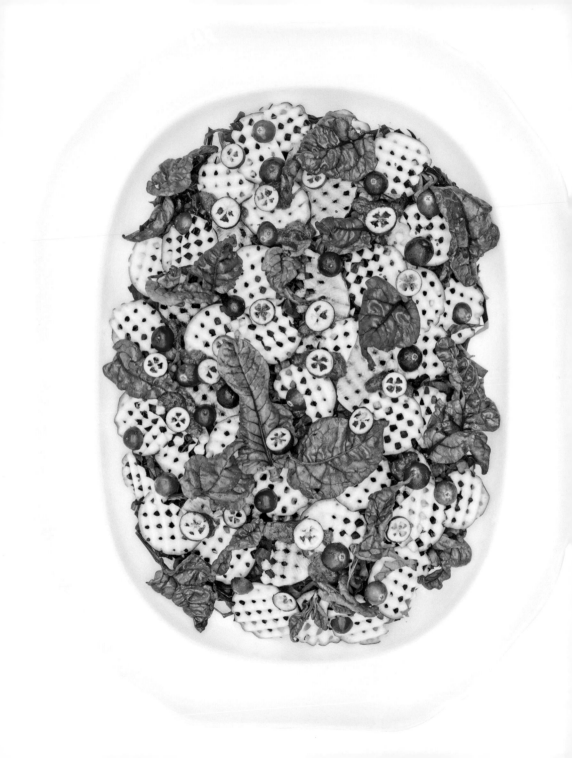

ZUCCHINI, CHARD & CRANBERRY SALAD

Fresh cranberries give such a festive feel to this salad. It would be the perfect Thanksgiving or Christmas side dish.

I've cut the zucchini into gaufrette-type slices using a serrated crinkle-cutter knife. First slice the zucchini one way then turn it 90 degrees and cut down to make a very thin slice, then turn it again 90 degrees to create a holey, waffle-cut slice. It takes some practice to get the checkerboard effect, but it's really satisfying when you achieve it. You could also use a mandoline.

1 large bunch of baby Swiss chard
2 to 3 large zucchini, trimmed
3 cups fresh cranberries, divided
3 tablespoons cranberry juice
1 teaspoon sumac
salt and pepper

You'll get plenty of potassium, vitamin A, and magnesium from this salad. And cranberries are packed with antioxidants and phytochemicals that could protect against urinary infections.

Tear the leafy parts of the chard away from the stems (save the stems for juicing) and chop finely. (The leaves have been left whole in the picture for decorative effect but are best finely chopped for eating.)

Slice (see the instructions above) or grate the zucchini and mix with the chard. Set aside 2 cups of the fresh cranberries to make a dressing and finely slice the rest (or leave some whole) and add to the chard and zucchini.

Place the reserved cranberries in a blender or food processor with the cranberry juice, 2 tablespoons water, sumac, and seasoning and blend to a smooth consistency. You may need to add some more water or cranberry juice to thin the dressing to a pouring consistency.

When you're ready to serve, pour the dressing evenly over the salad and toss well to coat all of the ingredients.

A festive twist . . .
This also makes a great post-Christmas or post-Thanksgiving salad with added diced roast squash, and toasted sourdough croutons.

VEGETABLE SALAD WITH FRESH MUSHROOMS

I love using fresh mushrooms in salads, but I find they can be a lot to eat in large quantities, especially in a salad made completely of mushrooms.

For that reason, I'll often mix mushrooms into a salad or use them as a topping as I've done in this dish, which is great for a party. The pomegranate seeds and edible flowers add an attractive finishing touch and the finely chopped rainbow chard stems give a mild, salty taste.

This salad is photographed without a dressing but the Asian-inspired Dressing (see page 131) or Pomegranate Vinaigrette (see page 127) would both be delicious.

Mushrooms contain B complex vitamins, which help us release energy from our food, plus copper—a mineral that contributes to normal immune function.

10½ to 14oz mushrooms
3 to 4 stems rainbow chard
2 to 3 large handfuls of grated or sliced vegetables, such as bell peppers, carrots, raw beets, or zucchini
1 handful of pomegranate seeds
edible flowers, to garnish
Asian-inspired Dressing (see page 131)
or Pomegranate Dressing (see page 127)

Thinly slice the mushrooms and very finely dice the stems of the rainbow chard.

Place the other grated and sliced vegetables on a large serving platter or in a bowl and scatter them with the sliced mushrooms.

Scatter the salad with the pomegranate seeds and diced rainbow chard stems and garnish with the edible flowers. Serve the salad with the dressing of your choice.

For a cooked alternative . . .
Roast the mushrooms whole and place on top before serving.

GREEN-ON-GREEN SALAD

This is a simple salad of peas, asparagus, fresh herbs, and fennel dressed simply in mandarin juice and a little seasoning. Asparagus is delicious raw, especially if it's really fresh, and you can cut it into beautiful dainty ribbons using just a vegetable peeler.

I used Sicilian green mandarins and their bracing sweet-sourness and almost herbal zest was all that the salad needed to moisten it and lift the grassy flavors. If you can't get hold of green mandarins, use oranges with a squeeze of lime.

Alternative, or additional, dressings would be a Lemony Salsa Verde (see page 133), Gremolata-style Dressing (see page 133), or the Green Juice Dressing (see page 128).

2 bunches of asparagus
1 large fennel bulb
2 cups freshly shelled peas
finely grated zest and juice of 2 to 3 Sicilian green mandarins
1 small bunch of mixed chopped herbs, such as mint, basil, dill, and parsley
salt and pepper

Your mom was right when she made you eat green vegetables. This salad is packed with folate, and the peas are rich in vitamin B_1 (thiamin), needed for a healthy nervous system.

Snap the woody ends off of the asparagus spears (the spears naturally yield and break in the right place when you bend them gently) and, using a vegetable peeler, cut them into ribbons.

Finely slice or shave the fennel and mix with the asparagus along with the peas. Combine the vegetables in a serving bowl or platter.

Sprinkle the salad with the mandarin zest and then squeeze the juice over it. Season the salad and scatter with the herbs to serve.

Hot extras . . .
Roasted chickpeas, cooked black beans, or roasted cauliflower florets would all be great additions.

SWISS CHARD & TOMATO SALAD

Swiss chard is great raw in salads because the leaves are so nutritious and pair well with all sorts of other flavors, while the naturally salty stems can be used finely chopped or juiced to make a dressing that doesn't need any extra salt.

It comes with a Tomato Dressing (see page 133), which is one of my favorite go-to dressings. You could reserve half of the cherry tomatoes intended for the dressing to scatter onto the salad, rather than use all of them in the dressing.

2 radicchio
2 bunches of Swiss chard
Tomato Dressing (see page 133)
½ cup pine nuts

The Swiss chard and tomato dressing combine to make this salad rich in vitamins and antioxidants. Pine nuts add a boost of magnesium—a mineral that's important for energy levels.

Finely shred the radicchio leaves and the leafy parts of the Swiss chard (you can juice the stems) and place them in a serving bowl.

Pour the tomato dressing evenly over the salad and scatter with the pine nuts just before serving.

Bulk it up . . .
A handful of crispy garlic croutons would add extra substance to this salad.

SWEET & SOUR VEGETABLE "NOODLES"

This light and lean salad is great to serve in the warmer months because it's crisp and refreshing with lots of vivid, zingy flavors. The Sweet & Sour Dressing is spicy and rich.

Sprouted seeds are widely considered to be one of nature's superfoods. You can buy them in most supermarkets but they're really easy to grow, too.

2 large carrots, scrubbed or peeled
2 zucchini, trimmed
1 large cucumber
3 to 4 scallions, trimmed
1 large red chile
½ red onion, peeled
1 large red bell pepper, seeded
1 large mango
2 tablespoons sesame seeds
1 handful of chopped cilantro
1 large handful of sprouted seeds or beansprouts

SWEET & SOUR DRESSING
2 tablespoons sesame oil
1 tablespoon date paste or sweetener of choice
1 teaspoon five-spice powder
2 teaspoons freshly grated ginger root
1 small garlic clove, peeled
finely grated zest and juice of 1 lime
1 teaspoon nama shoyu or soy sauce (optional)
salt and pepper

The sprouted seeds are the superfood ingredient in this salad, bursting with enzymes and vital nutrients, and they're also a source of raw plant-based protein.

Slice the carrots (there's no need to peel them if they are organic), zucchini, and cucumber into thin julienne strips or use a spiralizer to make vegetable "noodles."

Coarsely chop the scallions and finely chop the chile and red onion. Cut the red bell pepper and mango into small dice.

Place all the salad ingredients in a large bowl along with the sesame seeds, cilantro, and sprouted seeds or beansprouts and mix gently together (it's easiest to do this with your hands).

To make the dressing, place all the ingredients into the bowl of a food processor and blend to a smooth, thick consistency. If you prefer a more runny dressing, thin it down with a little extra lime juice or a splash of water. Season to taste.

Add the sweet and sour dressing to the salad and toss to coat.

Asian inspiration . . .

As an interesting alternative to rice or traditional noodles, you could serve the vegetable "noodles" with any Chinese-style sauce instead of the Sweet & Sour Dressing.

TOMATO & ARTICHOKE SALAD

Although you can eat the very young tender hearts of artichokes raw, if you can find a raw version of preserved artichokes (often bottled in olive oil) you may find them much tastier and less fiddly to prepare.

I've added some dehydrated tomatoes to this salad for a rich, tomato taste (see how to dehydrate your own on page 140), but you can use fresh ones instead.

The vibrant Orange Vinaigrette (see page 127) helps harmonize and enliven this salad.

2 red leaf lettuces
5½oz preserved artichoke hearts
Orange Vinaigrette (see page 127)
6 to 7 large dehydrated tomatoes, sliced
(see page 140), or sliced fresh tomatoes
1 small handful of basil leaves

This salad is rich in tomato lycopene and is a good source of vitamin C. Artichokes are used for maintaining liver health in traditional herbal medicine.

Tear the lettuce leaves into bite-sized pieces and place in a serving bowl or on a platter.

Chop the artichokes into coarse chunks (or leave whole, if you prefer).

Pour the orange vinaigrette evenly over the lettuce leaves, add the artichoke hearts and dehydrated or fresh tomatoes, and toss gently to coat. Finally, scatter with the basil, tearing up any larger leaves if needed, and serve.

Cooked extras . . .
Roasted vegetables would be in keeping with the Mediterranean feel of this salad.

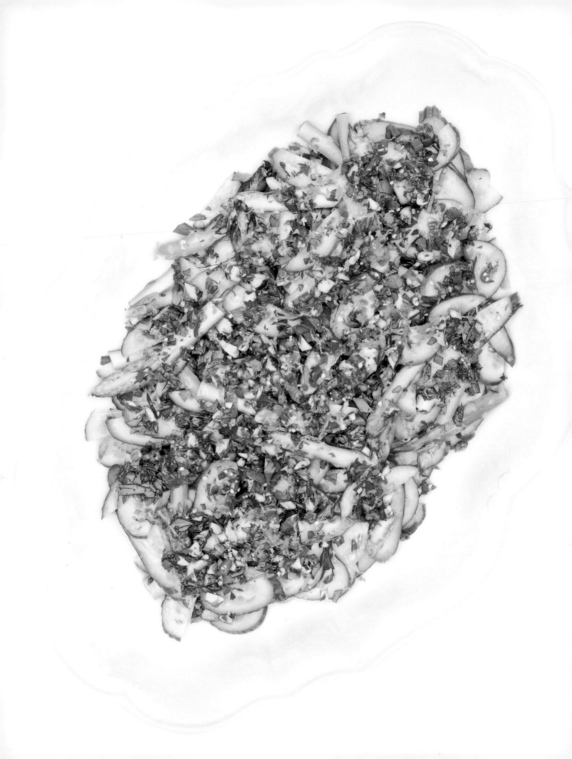

ASPARAGUS & CUCUMBER SALAD WITH SPICY ORANGE GREMOLATA

Thinly sliced asparagus and cucumber are sprinkled with a spicy orange gremolata, which adds both flavor and crunch to the vegetables.

Gremolata can have quite a dry texture, so it's great to use with more juicy salad ingredients because the combination of the two makes the gremolata more like a dressing in consistency.

6 to 7 asparagus spears, woody ends trimmed
2 large cucumbers

SPICY ORANGE GREMOLATA
2 red chiles, or to taste
1 small handful of parsley leaves
1¼ cups almonds or walnuts
1 orange
drizzle of cold-pressed extra virgin olive oil (optional)
salt and pepper

This salad is a good source of vitamin C, folate, and essential fats. The chiles will also give your metabolism a temporary boost.

Finely slice the asparagus and cucumbers and place in a serving bowl or on a platter.

To make the spicy orange gremolata, seed the chiles and place them on a cutting board with the parsley leaves and almonds or walnuts. Finely grate the orange zest over the ingredients on the cutting board and chop everything together (or do this in a food processor) until you have a fine mixture that still has some chunks in it.

Sprinkle the cucumber and asparagus with the gremolata and gently mix it in. Add a drizzle of olive oil, if you like, and a little seasoning.

CARROT "NOODLE" SALAD

Carrots are an ideal vegetable for spiralizing. They're fairly sturdy and can be prepared and dressed well in advance so they soften slightly by the time you want to eat them. I've used orange, yellow, and purple carrots and they make an attractive contrast in colors, if you can get hold of them.

Peanuts and carrots have a natural flavor affinity so I have teamed this salad with the Peanut Satay Dressing (see page 134) to echo that.

Eating carrots along with healthy fat of the peanut butter or tahini means you'll absorb more of the fat-soluble beta carotene (vitamin A) from the carrots.

3 to 4 large carrots, scrubbed or peeled
1 tablespoon poppy seeds
Peanut Satay Dressing (see page 134)
edible flowers, to garnish

Spiralize the carrots (there's no need to peel them if they're organic) into "noodles" or coarsely grate them using a box grater. Toss the carrots with the poppy seeds and arrange on a platter or place in a serving bowl.

Pour the peanut satay dressing evenly over the carrots, toss until combined, and top with a few edible flowers.

Protein boost . . .
Add a few handfuls of chopped spinach or toasted nuts and seeds.

RADICCHIO & BRUSSELS SPROUT SALAD

I'm a sucker for a salad colored pink and green!

The smaller inside leaves of a radicchio are often paler and more pink in color than the outer leaves and they look really pretty against the green of the Brussels sprouts.

Shaving the Brussels sprouts so they're wafer thin is a great way to incorporate them raw into a salad. If they are mixed in well, cabbage-phobic diners won't notice them.

This crunchy vibrant salad is great served with the Pistachio Pesto (see page 132) or Pomegranate Vinaigrette (see page 127).

2 radicchio
2 soft-leaf green lettuces
7oz Brussels sprouts
¾ cup pistachio kernels
Pistachio Pesto (see page 132) or
Pomegranate Vinaigrette (see page 127)
1 small handful of mixed chopped herbs, such as parsley,
dill, thyme, oregano, and basil

Brussels sprouts are little powerhouses of nutrition. They are rich in folate, vitamin C, and phytochemicals, which may reduce your cancer risk.

Tear the leaves of the radicchio and lettuce into bite-sized pieces.

Shave or slice the Brussels sprouts very finely and chop the pistachio kernels.

Combine all the ingredients together in a bowl, add the dressing of your choice, and serve scattered with the herbs.

For a cooked alternative . . .
Roast, grill, or sear the radicchio on a barbecue.
The outer leaves of the Brussels sprouts could be roasted until crisp.
For an extra protein element try marinated tempeh, or tofu.

APPLE "SPAGHETTI" WITH FALL FRUIT

I've spiralized the apples in this light autumnal salad to make "spaghetti" and then teamed them with black dessert grapes and golden-colored cubes of Sharon fruit. It comes with an aromatic and vibrant orange and passion fruit sauce.

I used grape leaves in this photo to give the recipe a truly autumnal feel, but don't include these in your salad.

3 large passion fruits
finely grated zest and juice of 1 orange
1 small bunch of seedless black grapes
juice of 1 lemon
3 large red-skinned apples
3 large Sharon fruit (Israeli persimmon)

Red-skinned apples are a good source of polyphenol antioxidants associated with a reduced risk of cardiovascular disease.

To make the sauce, halve the passion fruits, scoop out the flesh, and place in a bowl with the orange zest and juice. Mix everything together and chill until ready to serve.

While the sauce is chilling, pick the grapes from the stem and slice them in half.

Prepare an acidulated water bath to prevent the apple from discoloring. Squeeze the lemon juice into a large bowl filled with about 1 cup of cold water and set aside.

Make the apple "spaghetti" using a spiralizer or julienne peeler, or cut them into matchsticks. Place the prepared apples in the water bath and gently swirl them around so all the pieces are coated, then drain well on paper towels. Cut the Sharon fruit into dice.

To assemble the fruit salad, pile the apple spaghetti in the middle of a large bowl. Scatter it with the diced Sharon fruit and halved black grapes, then pour the orange and passion fruit sauce onto the salad.

Smooth servings . . .

Blend the fruit with coconut water to make a delicious dairy-free smoothie.

The Sharon fruit could be chargrilled or seared on a barbecue to give another flavor and texture to the salad.

Serve the fruit drizzled with vegan yogurt or light cream.

VEGETABLE "NOODLES" WITH COCONUT CURRY SAUCE

Although rich, this sauce has a fresh taste and can be gently warmed before serving, as can the "noodles": steam them, or plunge very briefly into boiling salted water and drain thoroughly, or lightly sauté in a wok or skillet.

2 green zucchini, trimmed
2 yellow zucchini, trimmed
1 large carrot, scrubbed or
    peeled
7oz sugar snap peas or
1½ cups freshly podded peas
2 cobs corn, outer husks
    removed
1 large handful of chopped
    mixed herbs, such
as cilantro, parsley, rosemary,
    oregano, and thyme
fresh coconut shavings and
lime wedges, to serve

COCONUT CURRY SAUCE
meat and milk from
1 fresh young coconut
(or 1 cup coconut milk,
1¼ cups coconut water, and
1¾ cups unsweetened
    desiccated coconut)
1 banana shallot, peeled
½ green chile
1 teaspoon grated ginger root
1 small garlic clove, peeled
finely grated zest and
juice of 1 lime
1 teaspoon medium-hot curry
    powder
1-inch piece fresh turmeric
or 2 teaspoons ground • • •
    turmeric
salt and pepper

The turmeric in this sauce has anti-inflammatory properties. Combining the spice with a good grating of fresh black pepper—rich in piperine—increases turmeric's bio-availability to your body.

Cut the green and yellow zucchini and carrot into long "noodles" using a julienne peeler or spiralizer. Cut the sugar snap peas into fine diagonal shreds and slice the corn kernels away from the cobs.

To make the sauce, blend together the meat and milk of the fresh coconut (or the coconut milk, coconut water, and desiccated coconut, if using) with the rest of the ingredients until creamy and silky smooth, then season to taste. (Juice the turmeric first if you are using the fresh root.)

Place all the vegetables in a large bowl, add the coconut curry sauce, and stir to combine.

Let the salad marinate for 30 minutes until the noodles soften slightly, then scatter with the chopped herbs and serve with shavings of fresh coconut (or you could use desiccated coconut) and wedges of lime for squeezing over.

SIMPLE CARROT SALAD

Carrots (like zucchini) can make an almost-instant salad and are a great hunger-assuager if you're ravenous when you get back home from work and need something to eat right away. I always keep a bottle of dressing in the fridge for such "emergencies" and after quickly grating a carrot or two I have a satisfying snack. This salad uses orange, yellow, and purple heirloom carrots, which I've mixed with a few lettuce leaves, chopped red cabbage, and fresh herbs.

A carrot salad is kind of a blank canvas when it comes to dressings as it teams with almost any type—spicy, fruity, creamy, or light—but my favorites are either the Orange Vinaigrette (see page 127) or Peanut Satay Dressing (see page 134) along with a topping of chopped nuts and golden raisins.

If you have organic carrots with their tops still on, reserve some of the green leaves to chop and scatter the salad with. They're also a good source of extra nutrients.

4 to 6 large carrots, preferably heirloom, scrubbed or peeled
¼ small red cabbage
1 small lettuce of choice
1 handful of mixed chopped soft-leaf herbs, such as parsley, dill, cilantro, and basil
dressing of choice

Carrots provide a fantastic source of beta carotene, which the body converts into vitamin A, needed for healthy eyes, skin, and the immune system. Carrot juice is also a great way to drink up the benefits of this vegetable. In fact, the creamy-sweet juice makes a good salad dressing in itself.

Chop, slice, or grate the carrots (if they're organic there's no need to peel them) and place them in a large bowl.

Finely chop the red cabbage and tear the lettuce into bite-sized pieces. Mix the vegetables into the carrots with the herbs.

Add your dressing of choice to the salad just before serving.

•
•
•
•

Raw and cooked . . .
Try combining both raw and cooked versions of the same vegetable in a salad. Here, you could add some roasted carrots for a spectrum of carrot-on-carrot flavors and textures.

ARUGULA & RADISH SALAD WITH SPIRULINA DRESSING

I've used Bangladeshi lemons in this recipe because I love
their ridged and crinkled green skin and bracing acidity.
I only come across them occasionally so a regular yellow
lemon is an adequate substitute.

14oz wild arugula leaves
1 watermelon radish or 3 to 4 regular radishes, trimmed
3 to 4 okra
1 large Bangladeshi lemon or regular lemon (optional)
Spirulina Dressing (see page 135), or sprinkling of spirulina
powder, or dressing of your choice

Spirulina is a blue-green
algae superfood, while
arugula is rich in iron,
folate, and vitamin A.

Scatter a large serving platter with the arugula or place it in a large
bowl. Finely slice the radish and okra and add to the arugula.

If you have a razor-sharp mandoline, you can slice the Bangladeshi
lemon microscopically thin so it's palatable raw, or just use the finely
grated zest and juice in the spirulina dressing and omit the
sliced lemon in the salad.

Pour the dressing over the salad or sprinkle it with a little of the
spirulina powder, as I have done here, and select a dressing
of your choice.

Sides and smalls . . .
This peppery arugula salad could be served in small portions as a palate cleanser
between courses.

WATERMELON & SUNFLOWER SEED SALAD

A vibrant summer salad for times when watermelons are at the peak of sweet, juicy ripeness and sunflowers are in full bloom.

Interestingly, you can eat almost every part of a sunflower at each stage of its life cycle. The sprouted seeds are fantastic in a salad and the petals used here give a mild, nutty taste in addition to the crunch of the seeds.

I've used red-veined sorrel because its slightly sour, acidic leaves balance the sweetness of the melon, but either spinach, or arugula with a squeeze of lemon, make good substitutes.

Watermelon flesh is made up of 92 percent water, so eating it is a refreshing way to quench your thirst in hot weather. The pink color comes from lycopene (also found in tomatoes), which has been associated with lowering the risk of cardiovascular disease.

1 large watermelon
1 large handful of sorrel leaves or baby spinach leaves
1½ cups sunflower seeds
petals from 3 to 4 sunflowers
salt and pepper

Smash up your watermelon and break it into bite-sized pieces, or cut it into large chunks, reserving any juices to use as a simple dressing.

Coarsely tear the sorrel or spinach leaves and mix with the watermelon in a large bowl or on a platter. Season to taste, adding some of the watermelon juices.

Scatter with the sunflower seeds and petals before serving.

For a great flavor combination . . .
At a barbecue, serve as a side salad, scattered with a handful of chopped fresh mint.

DRAGON FRUIT SALAD WITH PASSION FRUIT & CLEMENTINE DRESSING

Dragon fruit look beautifully surreal with their bright pink skin and soft green spikes. I've yet to find a way of detecting whether the flesh will be white or bright magenta pink, so every time I cut into one it's a surprise.

This tropical fruit salad with pineapple, pomelo, physalis (Chinese/cape gooseberry), and guava is dressed simply with a good squeeze of clementine juice and some passion fruit pulp. When fruit looks and tastes this good it doesn't need much else doing to it.

1 large pineapple
2 pomelo
2 to 3 guava
12 physalis
3 large dragon fruit
3 clementines
4 passion fruit
mint leaves, to decorate

Pineapples come second only to bananas as America's favorite fruit. A good source of Vitamin C, pineapples also have anti-inflammatory and digestive benefits, too.

Peel and core the pineapple and chop the flesh into chunks, then peel the pomelo and cut into segments.

Cut the guava in half and scoop out the flesh and remove the papery outside leaves from the physalis.

Remove the skin from the dragon fruit and chop into chunks or cut into shapes—I cut them into star shapes.

Arrange all the prepared fruit on a platter or place in a serving bowl. Cut the clementines in half and squeeze the juice all over the fruit salad. Cut the passion fruit in half and spoon their seedy pulp onto the salad too. Finally, scatter with a few fresh mint leaves to serve.

Skewers and smoothies . . .
As another way to present this salad, cut the fruit into bite-sized pieces and thread them onto skewers.
Blend the fruit with vegan yogurt and a handful of rolled or raw oats as a satisfying breakfast smoothie.

BELL PEPPER SALAD WITH CRUSHED TOMATO & ORANGE SALSA

The flavors of the bell peppers, oranges, and tomatoes go really well together and the colors look so cheerful. By mixing the oranges with tomatoes in the salsa you get a great sweet/salty/savory flavor combination, which is also delicious served with avocado.

4 to 5 red and orange bell peppers
1 handful of chopped mixed herbs, such as thyme, chives,
parsley, basil, and dill, plus extra to garnish

CRUSHED TOMATO & ORANGE SALSA
2 oranges
2 cups cherry tomatoes
3 scallions, trimmed
a splash of cold-pressed extra virgin olive oil
salt and pepper

Bell peppers and oranges are two of the richest sources of vitamin C, so eating this salad is beneficial for a strong immune system.

Seed and finely slice the bell peppers, sprinkling them with the chopped herbs as you add them to a serving bowl.

To make the salsa, cut away the peel and pith from the oranges and segment the flesh over a bowl to catch any juices, discarding the white membrane. Coarsely chop the orange segments.

Halve the tomatoes and press down gently on them to crush them and release their juices. Place the tomatoes and oranges in a bowl and scrape any remaining tomato juice from the cutting board into the bowl along with the reserved orange juice.

Finely chop the scallions and add to the tomato and oranges along with the olive oil and seasoning and stir gently together. The salsa is best left to stand at room temperature for an hour or so for the flavors to develop and mingle, but it can be served immediately.

When you're ready to serve, spoon the salsa over the pepper and herb mixture, and garnish with a few extra herbs.

Try this . . .
Avocado—plain, broiled, or baked until creamy—is the perfect addition to this salad.
Toasted sesame seeds would be delicious, too.

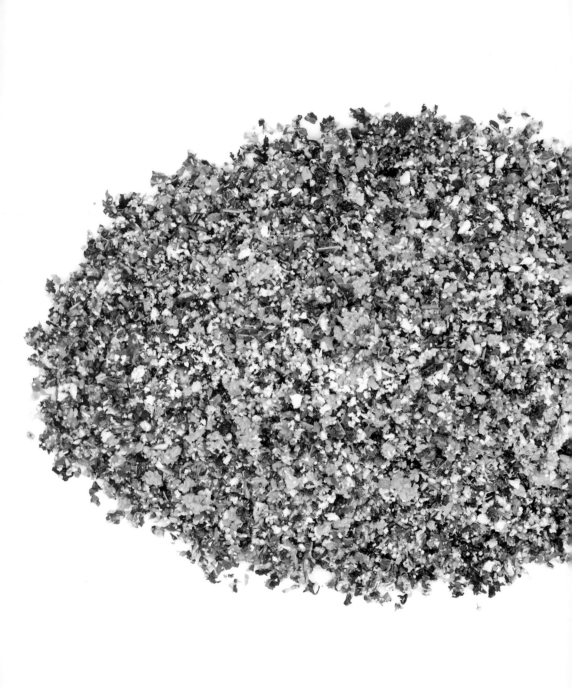

RAINBOW VEGETABLE "COUSCOUS"

Making a mixed vegetable "couscous" is a delicious way of using up any vegetables you have lurking in the fridge, and it makes a healthy low-carb alternative to traditional couscous.

I've used a spectrum of different colored fresh vegetables and blitzed them to an even-sized "grain" to give the same texture as couscous. I tend to process the different vegetables in separate batches to keep the colors distinct and then mix them together at the last minute.

Dry-textured vegetables are best so the grains keep separate and fluffy, but if you do use juicier vegetables just set them on paper towels after blitzing to absorb any moisture before mixing with the rest of the ingredients. Depending on which vegetables you use, this salad can be eaten on its own or dressed with vinaigrette.

2 to 3 bell peppers (red, orange, or yellow)
1 large sweet potato, peeled
5½oz baby corn
3 to 4 kale leaves
2 raw red or candy cane beets, scrubbed or peeled
2 large carrots, scrubbed or peeled
½ small red cabbage
½ head broccoli
1 small bunch of radishes, trimmed

The vibrant reds, yellows, and greens in this salad make it a rich source of the carotenoid antioxidants that help to protect skin and keep the immune system healthy.

Prepare the vegetables as needed then chop them into coarse chunks. Blitz the vegetables individually in a food processor to a fine, grainy texture. Be careful not to overprocess them or they will go mushy, and place the bell peppers on paper towels to absorb any excess moisture.

Tip all the blitzed vegetables into a large bowl and mix gently together with your hands or a large spoon to combine. Serve with or without a dressing of your choice.

If you like it hot . . .
Briefly sauté the "couscous" in a large wok or heat it in a microwave.
Serve instead of couscous or rice as an accompaniment.

ZUCCHINI BOLOGNESE

Spiralized zucchini has the same texture as cooked pasta but is low in carbs.
For pappardelle-style noodles, slice the zucchini into wide ribbons instead
of spiralizing them. If you don't like zucchini use carrots, cucumber, or
butternut squash instead. This dish is topped with a tomato-based sauce full
of lovely Mediterranean flavors, and finished with a sprinkling of cauliflower
"Parmesan". Soaked walnuts give the sauce a "meaty" texture.

4 zucchini, trimmed
3 to 4 small cauliflower florets

SAUCE
½ cup sun-dried tomatoes
4 Medjool dates
1 cup walnuts
1 carrot, scrubbed or peeled
½ raw red beet, scrubbed or
peeled
½ red onion, peeled
1 garlic clove, peeled

½ red chile
½ red bell pepper
1 celery stalk, trimmed
1 small handful of parsley
1 rosemary sprig
2¼ cups cherry tomatoes, divided
finely grated zest and juice of
1 lemon
2 handfuls of Greek basil leaves
(or use regular basil)
salt and pepper

Walnuts are a source
of vitamin E and the
omega-3 fat linolenic
acid, which can help
to maintain a healthy
cholesterol level.

Start the sauce a day early. Coarsely chop the sun-dried tomatoes and stone the
dates. Place both in a small bowl and add 1 cup water. Place the walnuts in a bowl and
add enough water to cover. Let both bowls stand in the fridge overnight.

The next day, coarsely chop the carrot, beet, onion, and garlic. Seed and finely chop
the chile and red bell pepper. Coarsely chop the celery, parsley, and rosemary leaves.
Chop ¼ cup of the cherry tomatoes into quarters and set aside.

Place the garlic, rosemary, and chile in the bowl of a food processor and blitz until
finely chopped. Add the carrot, celery, red bell pepper, and onion and blitz again.

Drain and rinse the walnuts and add to the other ingredients in the processor with
the beet, remaining fresh tomatoes, lemon zest and juice, soaked dates, and sun-dried
tomatoes (including their soaking water), parsley, and half the basil leaves. Process
the mixture until it forms a thick sauce and the walnut pieces resemble "ground
meat" in texture. Season to taste. Depending on how juicy the tomatoes
are, you may need to add a little extra water to thin the consistency of the sauce.

Spiralize the zucchini into long curly strands or slice into long thin strips using
a julienne or vegetable peeler.

Blitz the cauliflower florets in a processor until the texture of fine grains. If it contains
a lot of water, place the "Parmesan" on paper towels to soak up the moisture.

Arrange the spiralized zucchini on a large platter and pour the sauce evenly over
it. Scatter it with the reserved chopped tomatoes, cauliflower "Parmesan," and the
remaining basil leaves to serve.

For extra flavor . . .
Both the spiralized zucchini and the sauce can be heated up.

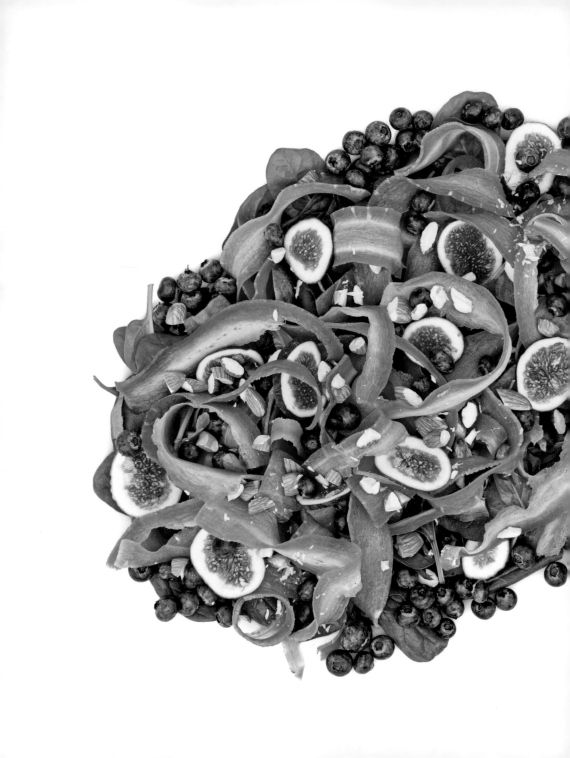

CARROT, FIG &
BLUEBERRY SALAD

I've left the blueberries whole in this salad, but you can
blend them with a little seasoning to make a vibrantly colored
fresh dressing instead of the Herb Vinaigrette
(see page 126) or Lemon Shallot Vinaigrette (see page 126).

To encourage the ribbons of carrot to curl, I've put them in
a bowl of iced water overnight. This is a great way of curling
any finely sliced vegetables and I often do it with scallions and
fennel because their spiky parts curl and contort into
all sorts of pretty shapes.

Carrots, almonds, figs,
spinach, and blueberries can
all legitimately be described
as superfoods. As an added
bonus, new research suggests
almonds aren't as calorific as
once thought—up to one-third
of their calories pass through the
digestive system unabsorbed.

3 to 4 large carrots, scrubbed or peeled
¾ cup whole almonds
5 figs
14oz baby spinach
1¼ cups blueberries
Herb Vinaigrette (see page 126) or
Lemon Shallot Vinaigrette (see page 126)

Using a vegetable peeler, cut the carrots into thin ribbons (there
is no need to peel them if they're organic) and either use them
immediately, or place in a bowl of cold water with ice cubes
overnight. (If using this method ensure that you drain the carrot
slices very well afterward and place them on some paper towels to
soak up any excess water before adding them to the salad.)

When you're ready to serve the salad, chop the almonds and
slice the figs.

Place the spinach in a bowl. Add the carrots, blueberries, figs, and
almonds. Pour the dressing of your choice on the salad to serve.

Try this...
You can roast the carrots in this salad instead of serving them raw and, for
additional protein, try marinated tempeh.

MANGO, BEET, KALE & RADISH SALAD

For this salad you can either chop the kale finely or break it into pieces and massage it in the mango dressing. It can get a little messy, but tastes delicious!

I've cut the yellow beet and pink watermelon radishes into decorative shapes for the photograph, but slice, grate, or shave them as you prefer.

If you'd like to serve a dressing with this salad, I recommend the Orange Vinaigrette (see page 127).

2 large bunches of kale
2 teaspoons cold-pressed extra virgin olive oil
3 ripe mangoes
1 large raw yellow beet, scrubbed or peeled
1 large watermelon radish or 5 to 6 regular radishes, trimmed
Orange Vinaigrette (see page 127) (optional)

Colorful vegetables tend to have plenty of vitamins and antioxidants, including lycopene, lutein, and vitamin C, so this salad is loaded with nutritients.

Tear the leafy parts of the kale away from the stems (save these for juicing) and remove any tough veins in the leaves. Tear the leaves into 1- to 2-inch pieces and place in a large bowl.

Anoint the kale leaves in the olive oil and start to massage and crush them with your fingers. It will take a while for the leaves to yield but they will gradually start to soften and become more pliable and tender. You'll know they're done when they feel silky soft.

Peel and seed the mangoes. If the mangoes are really ripe it's a good idea to massage them into the kale because they may be difficult to cut up neatly. Simply mash them up with your hands and get going.

Slice, grate, or shave the beet and watermelon radish, or cut into decorative shapes and scatter the salad with them just before serving. Dress the salad with the orange vinaigrette, if using.

Try this . . .
Roast the beet or make crispy chips from the kale to give an additional textural element to this salad.
A handful of cooked brown rice or quinoa would make a more substantial dish.

RED FRUIT SALAD

I love making salads of single or tonal colors and this platter of predominantly red fruit showcases some of the wonderful varieties available in the summer and early fall.

The fruit used here is fairly juicy so it doesn't really need a dressing, but you could squeeze the juice of 2 to 3 oranges onto it, if you like.

If you're making this salad ahead, layer the fruit in a bowl with the sturdiest ones, such as the grapes, on the bottom and the more fragile fruit, such as the red currants and strawberries, on top so they don't get crushed. Then just mix everything together gently before serving.

Fruits in the red/purple spectrum are rich in anthocyanin antioxidants, which can improve the strength and flexibility of the skin and blood vessels, and have anti-inflammatory qualities.

2¾ cups strawberries
2 cups red currants
1 small bunch of seedless black grapes
6 to 8 plums
4 ripe nectarines
1 cup raspberries
1¼ cups blackberries

Hull the strawberries and cut them in half.

Pick some of the red currants from the stem, leaving a few sprigs intact for decoration. Pick the grapes from their stem.

Remove the stones from the plums and nectarines and cut into thick slices or bite-sized pieces.

Arrange the fruit on a platter, decorating with the reserved red currant sprigs before serving.

Smooth alternatives . . .
The fruits in this salad would make a delicious juice or smoothie, blended together with or without vegan yogurt.

WATERMELON & CUCUMBER SALAD

This salad, with its refreshing flavors and the cooling textures of watermelon and cucumber, is particularly good in hot summer months. You can score the outside of the cucumber with a lemon zester to give it a decorative effect when sliced.

The red onion in this salad is rich in quercetin, which has natural anti-inflammatory and anti-histamine qualities. This is the salad to eat in the hay fever season.

1 small watermelon
1 large cucumber
½ red onion, peeled
1 small handful of mint sprigs
2 tablespoons raw apple cider vinegar
¼ teaspoon sumac
1 handful of microgreens or sprouted seeds
1 handful of garden cress
salt and pepper

Cut the melon in half and remove the seeds. Using a melon baller, scoop out small balls of melon or chop the flesh into chunks (reserve the juice to make a dressing).

Cut the cucumber in half lengthwise and scoop out and discard the seeds with a teaspoon, then slice the flesh into crescent shapes.

Very finely slice the red onion and pick the mint leaves from their stems.

To make a quick dressing, combine 3 to 4 tablespoons of the watermelon juice, the apple cider vinegar, sumac, and a little seasoning and beat together well.

Place the melon balls, cucumber slices, and red onion in a bowl, add the dressing, and use your hands to mix everything gently to combine. Finally scatter the salad with the microgreens or sprouted seeds and garden cress before serving.

Perfect pairings . . .
Chopped ripe tomatoes would add another dimension to this dish.

SNOWBERRY SALAD

This sweet salad is inspired by a dessert from the Ivy restaurant in London, where frozen berries were served with a warm white chocolate sauce.

My raw almond cream tastes chocolatey—in a white chocolate sort of way—since it's vanilla-flavored, creamy, and sweet. I make it using a high-speed blender and it's so rich, silky, and smooth, you wouldn't believe it isn't dairy cream! If you don't have a powerful blender use cashews instead as they're softer and blend to a smoother consistency more easily.

You may find the blending process results in a slightly warm cream that will start to thaw the berries as you pour it over them. For a warmer sauce, heat it in a small basin over a pan of gently boiling water.

For a superfood kick with a contrasting chewy texture and a little extra sweetness, scatter the salad with a few goji berries to finish.

Blackberries are packed with anthocyanins, which have antioxidant and anti-inflammatory properties.

1 small bunch of seedless grapes
2¼ cups red currants
2 cups raspberries
1¾ cups blackberries
2 tablespoons goji berries

RAW ALMOND CREAM
1½ cups almonds
6 Medjool dates, pitted
1 tablespoon organic virgin coconut oil
seeds from 1 vanilla bean

It's best to start this dish a day before you need it so the berries can freeze properly but, saying that, they're also lovely served semifrozen after a couple of hours in the freezer, so choose whichever method you fancy.

You can also start to make the raw almond cream ahead by soaking the nuts overnight in water, and soaking the dates separately in 2 cups of water.

Wash and dry the fresh fruit well and pick the grapes and red currants from their stems, leaving a few red currant sprigs intact to decorate.

Open-freeze the fruit by spreading it out on a baking pan or tray lined with parchment paper and placing it in the freezer. This freezing method keeps the fruit separate and undamaged.

To make the raw almond cream, drain and rinse the soaked almonds then blend with the other ingredients (including the soaking water from the dates) until smooth and creamy. Add a little more water if the cream looks too thick.

Tip the frozen berries onto a platter (avoid handling them to protect their frosted coating), drizzle with the almond cream, and scatter with the goji berries to serve.

.
.
.
●

Smooth and cool alternatives . . .
Turn this salad into a fruit-filled smoothie with a little water or coconut water, or freeze into ice pops.

CONFETTI FRUIT PLATTER WITH AN ORANGE & MANGO DRESSING

This is not a recipe so much as a suggestion for presenting a wonderful platter of fruity ingredients. I love to serve fruit on a big communal platter so people can help themselves.

I've used different cutting techniques and tools to create the various shapes and effects: two different sizes of melon baller (a standard and a mini ¼-inch one) were used to make the melon and papaya balls, and an ice-cream scoop to shape the large melon curls. I've cut the kiwi fruit into zig-zag halves by making a serrated cut around the equator of the fruit and pulling the two halves apart. The Sharon fruit is simply diced, while the plums are sliced.

The platter is finished with a scattering of yellow rose petals and finely chopped fuchsias.

The orange and mango together make a beautiful bright orange, silky-smooth sauce, which is lovely poured onto chopped fresh fruit. Or, you could try it with the Apple "Spaghetti" with Fall Fruit (see page 92).

This fruity bonanza isn't just delicious—one serving will also provide you with most of the vitamins and minerals you will need for the day.

2 large white Asian pears
2 muskmelons
1 pomegranate
1 papaya
1 Sharon fruit (Israeli persimmon)
3 plums
3 to 4 kiwi fruit
2 nectarines
1 handful of edible flowers, to decorate

ORANGE & MANGO DRESSING
2 ripe mangoes
finely grated zest and juice of 1 large orange
3 Medjool dates, pitted
2 tablespoons coconut water

Slice, dice, scoop, and prepare your fruit selection as you wish, then arrange everything artistically on a platter.

For the dressing, peel, seed, and dice the mangoes. Add to a blender with the rest of the ingredients and process until smooth.

Scatter with a few edible flowers as a finishing touch—beautiful!

- Smooth and cool alternatives . . .
- Blend the fruit for an exotic-tasting smoothie, or freeze the blended fruit to make a sorbet or granita.

SCARLET SLAW

This festive slaw is made with winter fruit and vegetables and served with a Citrus & Beet Dressing (see page 128), which turns the salad a gorgeous shade of scarlet. The salad keeps really well in the fridge for up to 4 to 5 days and is even better for doing so as the flavors get a chance to mingle and develop.

This slaw is packed with cruciferous vegetables, anti-oxidant-rich cranberries, and blood pressure-lowering beets.

½ Savoy cabbage
9 oz Brussels sprouts
1 handful of flat-leaf parsley
6 to 8 kumquats
1 red onion, peeled
3 small carrots, scrubbed or peeled
2 large Braeburn apples
juice of 1 lemon
1 handful of dried cranberries
Citrus & Beet Dressing (see page 128)

Finely shred the cabbage and Brussels sprouts by either cutting them very, very finely or using the shredding disk on a food processor.

Coarsely chop the parsley and finely slice the kumquats and red onion. Slice the carrots crossways into thin disks (there's no need to peel them if they are organic).

Cut the apples into matchsticks then toss them in the lemon juice to stop them from discoloring.

To assemble the salad, gently toss all the ingredients together, including the cranberries, in a large bowl. Pour the citrus and beet dressing evenly over the ingredients and mix gently again. If you decide to keep it for a few days covered in the fridge, mix again before serving to combine.

PASSION FRUIT SLAW

This salad is full of fresh, crisp natural goodness, while
the Passion Fruit Dressing (see page 128) lends a tropical
sweetness. The longer you let the salad marinate
in the dressing, the softer and more pliable the shredded
raw vegetables will become.

1 pointed cabbage
2 celery stalks, trimmed
3 large asparagus spears, woody ends removed
3 scallions, trimmed
1 carrot, scrubbed or peeled
1 large green apple
Passion Fruit Dressing (see page 128)
salt and pepper
extra passion fruit pulp and finely
shredded scallions, to serve

This dish is high in fiber
and vitamin C—an
important immune system
nutrient all year round,
but especially during the
cold and flu season.

Finely slice the cabbage, celery, asparagus, and scallions
and grate the carrot and apple, discarding the core. Toss the
ingredients together in a large bowl.

Pour the passion-fruit dressing evenly over the salad, mix well, and
season to taste. Eat immediately or cover and refrigerate for 1 to
2 days to let the slaw soften slightly and to allow the flavors to
meld and develop.

Mix well before serving, adding a few extra spoonfuls of passion-fruit
pulp and scattering the slaw with a few finely shredded scallions.

KALE SLAW

When I was young, kale was often grown as cattle feed but now not many people need convincing of the nutritional power of the mighty kale! My favorite variety is cavolo nero (dino kale), which is great juiced, blended into a smoothie, or massaged into silky submission in a salad. But I can never resist the more decorative types of kale too—the pink, purple, white, and frilly-edged varieties sometimes look so unreal.

In this slaw, I've shredded the leaves and very finely chopped the tender parts of the stems before mixing them with a handful of grapes.

The ingredients are robust enough to handle almost any favorite dressing but I like to use the Grilled Citrus Dressing (see page 129) or Pomegranate Vinaigrette (see page 127).

Kale is absolutely packed with an antioxidant called lutein, which protects the back of the eye from UV damage. Studies suggest eating it regularly could protect against age-related macular degeneration.

1 big bunch of kale of choice, such as cavolo nero
2 large handfuls of seedless black grapes
Grilled Citrus Dressing (see page 129) or Pomegranate Vinaigrette (see page 127).

Tear the leaves away from the stems of the kale and very finely chop or thinly slice them (a chiffonade-type cut works well on any large or broad kale leaves).

To prepare the kale stems, tear the tender parts away from the hard, woodier stems (reserving these for juicing) and very, very, finely chop the tender stems.

Combine the kale leaves and stems with the grapes in a large bowl and add the dressing of your choice.

Sweet sippers . . .
Try juicing the kale and grapes together (the sweetness of the grapes curbs any bitterness in the kale), for a "liquid" salad.

PAPAYA SLAW SALAD

This fruity coleslaw is made with two types of cabbage to add different textures, as well as papaya, nectarines, parsley, and scallions. For extra crunch with good staying power (it doesn't get soggy), add a couple of handfuls of beansprouts.

This salad travels well so it makes good picnic fare, or if you want to make it in advance to serve at a barbecue or buffet. The juices from the fruit make their own kind of dressing, but if you want to add a traditional creamy slaw-type dressing then the Ranch Dressing with Herbs (see page 130) or Raw Cashew Mayo (see page 131) are both suitable.

1 Savoy cabbage
1 to 2 small pointed cabbages
1 handful of flat-leaf parsley
3 to 4 scallions, trimmed
1 large papaya
2 to 3 ripe nectarines
a pinch of dried red chile flakes (optional)
salt and pepper

This salad will give you a boost of vitamin C (papayas contain more than oranges). Savoy cabbage supplies bone-friendly calcium, too.

Finely shred the cabbages and finely chop the parsley and scallions, then put everything in a large bowl.

Halve, peel, and seed the papaya and remove the stones from the nectarines. Chop both fruit into small dice and add to the bowl with the rest of the ingredients, saving any juices from the fruit to make a simple dressing.

Combine all the ingredients in the bowl with the red chile flakes and reserved juices and season to taste. Chill for 30 minutes before serving to allow the cabbage to soften and the flavors to develop.

. . .

Try this . . .
Chargrilled vegetables would all make a great addition to this salad.

dressings

SALAD DRESSINGS

Homemade salad dressings taste so much better than ready-made brands. And not only do you know exactly what's in them, you can tweak the ingredients to suit the flavors of the salad you're making.

Dressings don't have to be complicated. Sometimes, a drizzle of good cold-pressed extra virgin olive oil or a simple squeeze of lemon or lime juice is all that you need. For more elaborate salads, a luxurious flavorsome emulsion or brightly colored dressing is the way to take a bowl of leafy goodness to another level. A good dressing can unify the different flavors and textural elements of your salad to give it cohesiveness.

Depending on how you're using them, dressings can be served at any temperature—hot, warm, room temperature, cold, or even iced—and any recipe for a sauce, salsa, or dip can be thinned down and turned into a great dressing. You can make dressings with very simple or complex flavor combinations and also have fun

with color. Fresh turmeric makes a beautiful, vivid yellow dressing, spirulina a vibrant electric green, beet adds bright magenta tones, and blackberries and blueberries make a wonderfully sinister, darkly colored dressing.

A dressing can be used to enhance the other ingredients in your salad, as a counterbalance, or in contrast. So, you can also experiment with different flavorings—fresh, light, spicy, acidic, creamy, or rich—and unusual combinations, such as the Spirulina Dressing (see page 135). Or, you could try my quirky suggestion for Coffee Vinaigrette (see page 127). It has an intriguing bitter note that works brilliantly with robustly flavored greens, roasted vegetables, or anything with chiles.

It's also possible to vary the texture of your dressings (smooth vs chunky) and the consistency (thick vs thin), depending on the kind of salad your dressing is going with (robust leaves/chunky cut vs delicate leaves/finely cut). Just bear in mind the prevalent textures and flavors of your salad and dress it accordingly. I also sometimes

like to double-dress a salad by first coating the leaves in a light vinaigrette and then adding a second heavier, more robustly flavored dressing. It may sound a little "over the top," but it's a good way to add depth of flavor and interest to a simple bowl of leaves.

TO DRESS OR NOT TO DRESS?

To serve your salad dressed or bare but with a dressing on the side, is often a matter of personal preference, practicality, and timing.

Some salads, such as coleslaws or ones made with starchy vegetables like carrots, sweet potatoes, and squash, benefit from predressing, whereas soft leafy salads wilt quickly in a dressing so should be dressed just before serving. Other salads that contain "juicy" ingredients, such as fruit, may not need a dressing at all. Go with your personal preference and experiment with different ideas.

MAKING A BASIC VINAIGRETTE

My go-to dressing is always vinaigrette. I use a basic recipe and just add to it depending on what I have on hand, what flavor I am in the mood for, and the type of salad I'm making. I normally use a 3:1 ratio of oil to acid, but may go with 1:1 to keep the fat content lower (it seems to emulsify just as well). For my base recipe, see the Mothership Vinaigrette on page 126.

A vinaigrette dressing starts with an oil element and an acid element. These are the ones I most frequently use in my dressings:

❋ **Acid:** vinegar (usually raw apple cider vinegar or balsamic vinegar), citrus juice, or other fruit and vegetable juices including beet, tomato, or celery.

❋ **Oil:** cold-pressed extra virgin olive oil, coconut oil, canola oil, flavored oils such as lemon oil, avocado oil, chile oil, sesame seed oil, or walnut oil, and oil from bottled preserved fruit and vegetables, such as sun-dried tomatoes or roasted bell peppers.

FLAVORING A DRESSING

When I've made my base Mothership Vinaigrette (see page 126), I then add ingredients to create the flavor profile I'm looking for, and that will best suit the salad I'm making. These may be:

❋ **Sweet:** date paste or other sweeteners (stevia, agave syrup, maple syrup, coconut sugar), pomegranate molasses, balsamic vinegar, chutney/jam, coconut sugar, fruit, caramelized onions, sun-dried tomatoes, fresh fruit and berries, dried fruit, or sweet pickles.

❋ **Salty:** sea salt, flavored salts, soy sauce or the equivalent, such as nama shoyu, coconut aminos, or tamari, salty vegetables, like celery, tomatoes, Swiss chard stems, or seaweed (fresh or dried).

❋ **Sour:** citrus juice such as lemon, lime, or orange, lemon grass, rhubarb, vegan yogurt, extra vinegar, fermented foods such as kimchi, kombucha or sauerkraut.

❋ **Spicy/piquant:** mustard, chile, fresh ginger root, garlic, harissa, horseradish, or wasabi.

❋ **Bitter:** coffee, cacao, grapefruit juice, yuzu juice, or beer.

❋ **Umami:** sun-dried tomatoes, seaweed (fresh or dried), miso, or dried porcini mushrooms.

You can then use my flavor suggestions, above, to balance and enhance the taste of your dressing, remembering that:

❋ **Salty and umami flavors:** balance bitterness and enhance sweetness.

❋ **Sour flavors:** balance spice and sweetness, and enhance saltiness.

❋ **Sweet flavors:** balance sour and bitterness, and enhance saltiness.

❋ **Bitter flavors:** balance sweetness and saltiness.

❋ **Spicy flavors:** balance sour and sweet.

So, for example, if you have a salad made up of predominantly bitter radicchio or slightly spicy arugula, choose a dressing with a little sweetness. If you have a sweet-tasting, fruit-based salad, choose a dressing with a little sourness or salt. For example, ripe watermelon dressed with lime juice and a little salt is flavor-balanced perfection!

MIXING A DRESSING

There are various ways to mix a dressing. If it's a basic vinaigrette, I usually just whisk everything together in a large measuring cup. Some dressings may benefit from a different method of mixing:

❋ shake to emulsify in a screw-top jar

❋ combine in a food processor or blender (oil-based dressings emulsify best this way when the oil is trickled in slowly)

❋ grind in a mortar and pestle (or smash for chunkier dressings)

❋ juice (for thin, pure vegetable- or fruit-based dressings)

❋ add individual dressing ingredients, one by one, to the salad in the bowl to be tossed together before serving

❋ chop ingredients together on a board (for a chunky dressing)

Bear in mind that you'll get a different texture depending on whether you use a blender or a food processor. The latter slices and chops the ingredients so you get a coarser texture, whereas a blender breaks them down into a smooth or almost smooth sauce depending on how long you blend them for.

Another one-bowl method is to make the dressing in the salad bowl then take your serving utensils, cross them in the bowl and pile your salad leaves on top until ready to serve. The utensils will suspend the leaves above the dressing, keeping them crisp until it's time to toss everything together.

Oil

WAYS TO APPLY A DRESSING

There are several ways to dress a salad and I find the best way for most leafy mixed salads is to simply use your hands to gently mix or toss them in the dressing. That way you can feel when everything is evenly coated. Other types of salad benefit from different methods, including:

❋ drizzling the dressing evenly on top

❋ massaging it into the leaves (particularly good with thick leaves such as kale)

❋ dolloping it on top, like splotches of paint (good if it's a thick, heavy dressing)

❋ spraying it onto the salad using a fine misting bottle or spray

❋ squirting it from a plastic bottle, Jackson Pollock-style!

❋ predressing your salad before serving (particularly good for slaws)

❋ drizzling it in layers, interspersing the dressing with the salad ingredients

❋ serving it molecular gastronomy-style with "caviar pearls" containing the dressing, so when you bite into the salad the pearl gently bursts, releasing the dressing

❋ freezing it, granita-style, then shave the iced dressing over the top of the salad

DRESSING TIPS

❋ Most homemade dressings will keep for up to 1 week sealed in an airtight jar in the fridge. I also freeze dressings in small resealable plastic food bags or ice-cube trays with great success.

❋ I like to keep a jar of dressing in the fridge so I can put something together to eat in minutes. Simply pour some dressing onto prepared leaves or a pile of grated carrots or zucchini, for instance, and you have a nutritious, almost-instant, hunger assuager.

❋ If you have a slow juicer, try juicing a whole unwaxed, organic lemon—it gives a dressing the most amazing citrus flavor.

❋ If using citrus juice in a dressing, don't waste the zest (if organic and unwaxed). It has so much flavor! Finely grate the zest and freeze it if you don't have any immediate use for it.

❋ A peeled garlic clove placed in a jar of dressing for a few hours (or up to 1 week in the fridge) will give a lovely subtle flavor.

❋ Give your vinaigrette a different texture: try whisking it with an aerolatte milk frother to create a hollandaise-type dressing.

❋ Finally, don't forget to season your dressing and adjust the flavor profile to suit the ingredients of your salad.

Acid

Salty

Umami/Savory

Extra flavorings

Bitter

Sweet

MOTHERSHIP VINAIGRETTE

This is my basic vinaigrette recipe. I use a 3:1 ratio of oil to acid, unless I'm cutting back on fat and then I'll use a 1:1 ratio, or no oil at all. Then I blitz it in a food processor to help emulsify the ingredients.

2 tablespoons orange, lemon, or pink grapefruit
juice, or raw apple cider vinegar, or balsamic vinegar
1 tablespoon finely grated citrus zest
1 to 2 teaspoons maple syrup,
or 2 pitted Medjool dates (soaked until soft),
or sweetener of choice
1 to 2 teaspoons wholegrain mustard
1 small handful of mixed herbs, such as parsley,
mint, thyme, marjoram, chives, basil, tarragon,
and dill (or you could use individual herbs rather
than a mixture)
6 tablespoons cold-pressed extra virgin olive oil
salt and pepper

Blitz all the ingredients, except the olive oil, together in a food processor.

Gradually trickle in the olive oil through the funnel while the motor is still running. After a minute or two the ingredients should have emulsified and thickened. Taste and add seasoning. Seal the dressing in an airtight jar and store in the fridge for up to 2 weeks.

VARIATIONS

✳ **Tarragon Vinaigrette:** instead of using a combination of herbs add 2 tablespoons chopped tarragon and combine with the rest of the ingredients in the Mothership Vinaigrette.

✳ **Herb Vinaigrette:** instead of using a combination of herbs, add 2 tablespoons of a combination of chopped herbs of your choice and combine with the rest of the ingredients, above.

✳ **Cherry Vinaigrette:** instead of the mixed herbs use 1 cup fresh pitted sweet cherries with the rest of the ingredients, above.

✳ **Lemon Shallot Vinaigrette:** use 2 to 3 tablespoons lemon juice, 1 tablespoon finely grated lemon zest, and 1 finely chopped shallot with the rest of the ingredients, above.

Top to bottom:
Pomegranate Vinaigrette, Coffee Vinaigrette,
Sweet Smoky Paprika Vinaigrette.

POMEGRANATE VINAIGRETTE

This sweet-sour dressing is perfect with more robust salads such as the Kale Slaw (see page 120), the Radicchio & Brussels Sprout Salad (see page 91), or the Vegetable Salad with Fresh Mushrooms (see page 79).

1 tablespoon pomegranate molasses
or 3 tablespoons pomegranate juice
1 tablespoon red wine vinegar
2 tablespoons cold-pressed extra virgin olive oil
1 teaspoon date paste or sweetener of choice
2 tablespoons pomegranate seeds
salt and pepper

Blend together all the ingredients except the pomegranate seeds until smooth. Stir in the pomegranate seeds and season just before serving.

COFFEE VINAIGRETTE

This unusual vinaigrette works brilliantly with robustly flavored greens or roasted vegetables, or with any salad that includes walnuts, chiles, or beef.

1 teaspoon espresso powder or ground espresso
2 tablespoons cold-pressed extra virgin olive oil
2 teaspoons red wine vinegar
1 teaspoon date paste or sweetener of choice
salt and pepper

Whisk together all the ingredients until the espresso powder dissolves, or if you're using ground espresso let the dressing sit for at least 30 minutes, or overnight, to allow the flavors to develop. Strain the dressing, discarding the coffee grounds, and season before serving. Garnish with whole coffee beans, if you wish.

ORANGE VINAIGRETTE

This zesty, vibrant dressing enlivens the Tomato & Artichoke salad (see page 85). For a more subtle hint of garlic, place the whole clove in the dressing for 10 to 20 minutes, rather than grating it in.

2 tablespoons cold-pressed extra virgin olive oil
finely grated zest and juice of 1 orange
1 small garlic clove, peeled
salt and pepper

Whisk together the olive oil, orange zest and juice, and some seasoning, then finely grate in the garlic.

SWEET SMOKY PAPRIKA VINAIGRETTE

Smoked paprika lends a real depth of flavor to this dressing. You could serve it with the Frisée & Fig Salad (see page 67) or any carrot-based salad. And it's lovely with couscous, quinoa, or roasted vegetables, too.

1 shallot, peeled
1 small rosemary sprig
2 tablespoons cold-pressed extra virgin olive oil (or oil from a jar of roasted bell peppers)
1 tablespoon red wine vinegar
1 teaspoon sweet smoked paprika
a pinch of dried red chile flakes
salt

Finely chop the shallot and the leaves from the rosemary sprig, then whisk together with the rest of the ingredients until combined. Season to taste.

CITRUS GINGER DRESSING

Adding fresh ginger root to a dressing gives it a warm, spicy flavor, and when combined with citrus it makes a great winter-cold buster. Team this dressing with the Fig & Pomegranate Salad (see page 29).

2 large carrots, scrubbed or peeled
½-inch piece fresh ginger root, peeled
1 small shallot, peeled
juice of 1 lime
salt and pepper

Put the carrots, ginger, and shallot in a high-speed blender with the lime juice and 2 tablespoons water and process until smooth and creamy. Season to taste.

PASSION FRUIT DRESSING

This dressing gives a tropical sweetness and crunch to salads. It's especially good with the Passion Fruit Slaw (see page 119).

3 passion fruits
finely grated zest and juice of 1 large orange
2 tablespoons cold-pressed extra virgin olive oil
1 tablespoon poppy seeds
salt and pepper

Spoon the pulp from the passion fruits into a bowl. Whisk together the orange zest, juice, and olive oil, then stir into the passion fruit pulp with the poppy seeds. Season to taste.

CITRUS & BEET DRESSING

I love this earthy, fruity, vibrant dressing on the Scarlet Slaw (see page 118) as well as the Frisée & Fig Salad (see page 67).

1 large raw beet, scrubbed or peeled
4 to 5 clementines, peeled
finely grated zest of 1 lemon
salt and pepper

Juice the beet and clementines and combine with the lemon zest and a little seasoning. (If you don't have a juicer, you could coarsely grate the beet and stir it into your salad—the color will gradually bleed beautifully into the other ingredients to give the same effect. Then simply squeeze the clementine juice over the salad and sprinkle with the lemon zest and seasoning.)

MAPLE, LEMON & GINGER DRESSING

The slight sweetness of this dressing goes really well with bitter leaves or more robust creations, such as the Sweet Potato & Pea Salad (see page 73).

2 Meyer lemons, juiced whole, or 1 regular unwaxed lemon mixed with 1 unwaxed mandarin/clementine
3 small shallots, peeled
1 heaped teaspoon wholegrain mustard
1 to 2 teaspoons maple syrup or sweetener of choice
$\frac{1}{2}$-inch piece fresh ginger root, peeled
1 to 2 tablespoons cold-pressed extra virgin olive oil
a pinch of dried red chile flakes
salt and pepper

Blend all the ingredients together in a food processor until thick and emulsified. Season to taste.

GREEN JUICE DRESSING

Freshly made green juice is a wonderful oil-free dressing. Omit the garlic if you don't like it raw or substitute chives, scallion, or shallot for a milder onion flavor. In keeping with the green theme, serve it with the Green-on-Green Salad (see page 81).

1 large cucumber
1 small bunch of parsley, basil, or cilantro
1 handful of dark leafy greens, such as kale, spinach, or Swiss chard
1 Romaine or 2 to 3 Little Gem lettuces
1-inch piece fresh ginger root, peeled
juice of 1 lemon
$\frac{1}{4}$ garlic clove, peeled
salt and pepper

Put all the ingredients through a juicer, or blend in a food processor with ½ cup of water. (If blending, strain the juice through a sieve before serving.) Season and use within 30 minutes of making for maximum nutritional benefit.

Left to right: Grilled Citrus Dressing, Roasted Red Bell Pepper Dressing, Citrus & Beet Dressing, Passion Fruit Dressing, Green Juice Dressing.

ROASTED RED BELL PEPPER DRESSING

Bell peppers take on a smoky sweetness after roasting and when blitzed with garlic, basil, and lemon, make a magical dressing that works with fresh or cooked vegetables. Try this with the Little Gem "Tacos" (see page 49) instead of the avocado and bell pepper salsa, or with the Edamame Bean Salad (see page 57).

4 to 5 large roasted red or orange bell peppers
(or use ones from a jar)
1 small garlic clove, peeled
1 small handful of basil leaves
juice of 1 lemon
salt and pepper

Blend together all the ingredients in a food processor or blender until smooth and creamy. Season to taste.

ROSE HARISSA DRESSING

Rose harissa has a beautiful flavor of sweet smoked chile, spices, and rose petals. This dressing is superb for salads, and in soups, couscous, quinoa, rice, or pasta dishes. Use instead of the dressing in the Sweet & Sour Vegetable "Noodles" (see page 84) or on the Vegetable Salad with Fresh Mushrooms (see page 79).

1 tablespoon rose harissa paste
2 tablespoons cold-pressed extra virgin olive oil
1 tablespoon red wine vinegar
1 teaspoon maple syrup or sweetener of choice
salt and pepper

Blend all the ingredients to combine and season to taste.

GRILLED CITRUS DRESSING

Citrus fruit takes on a wonderful flavor when roasted, or grilled on a barbecue, as the juices become sweeter and give the dressing a delicate smoky taste. This dressing is also delicious with a few cloves of crushed roasted garlic blended in. Use this to dress the Avocado "Truffle" Salad (see page 27) or the Kale Slaw (see page 120).

2 large oranges, halved
2 lemons, halved
$\frac{1}{3}$ cup cold-pressed extra virgin olive oil
1 teaspoon Dijon or wholegrain mustard
1 teaspoon maple syrup or sweetener of choice
salt and pepper

Place the citrus fruit halves cut-side down on a hot barbecue, or cut-side up on a baking pan under a hot broiler, until they start to brown and caramelize. Remove from the heat. When cool enough to handle, squeeze the juice and flesh into a bowl.
Add the rest of the ingredients and beat or blend to form an emulsified dressing. Season to taste.

SUN-DRIED TOMATO DRESSING

Sun-dried tomatoes add a great depth of savory umami flavor. They add a rich tomato taste to the Avocado, Tomato & Lettuce Salad (see page 38), and their sweetness combines well with the natural saltiness of the Bok Choy & Samphire Salad (see page 28).

1 cup sun-dried tomatoes in oil
3 tablespoons cold-pressed extra virgin olive
oil (or oil from the jar of sun-dried tomatoes)
1 teaspoon wholegrain mustard
1 teaspoon date paste or sweetener of choice
2 tablespoons light balsamic vinegar
1 teaspoon sweet smoked paprika
salt and pepper

Blend together all the ingredients in a food processor until combined but still slightly chunky. Season to taste.

SWEET CHILE & LEMON DRESSING

This dressing gives a sweet, spicy, sour note to salads. Serve it with the Green-on-Green Salad (see page 81) or Cauli-flower Salad (see page 45). For a spicy kick, add a finely chopped fresh red chile.

1 scallion, trimmed
2 tablespoons sweet chili sauce or chile pepper jelly
1 tablespoon lemon juice or raw apple cider vinegar
2 tablespoons cold-pressed extra virgin olive oil
salt and pepper

Finely chop the scallion and whisk together with the rest of the ingredients. Season to taste.

RANCH DRESSING WITH HERBS

Dairy-free, rich, and creamy, this dressing, enhanced with herbs, teams well with the Kale Slaw (see page 120), Simple Carrot Salad (see page 95), or Crunchy Carrot & Beet Salad (see page 53) as an alternative to the Raw Cashew Mayo.

1½ cups cashews
finely grated zest and juice of 1 large lemon
1 scallion (white part only)
1 teaspoon date paste or sweetener of choice
a pinch of cayenne pepper
2 teaspoons walnut oil
1 small handful of chopped mixed herbs, such as chives,
parsley, dill, basil, and cilantro
salt and pepper

Soak the cashews for about 8 hours, or overnight, until softened, to make them easier to blend to a creamy consistency.

Drain the cashews and add to a high-speed blender along with the lemon zest and juice, the white part of the scallion, the date paste, cayenne pepper, walnut oil, and 1 cup of water. Blend until smooth and creamy.

Add more water to the dressing if you prefer a thinner consistency, stir in the chopped herbs, and season to taste.

RAW CASHEW MAYO

Rich and creamy, this raw cashew mayonnaise is perfect on
thinly sliced, crisp fresh vegetables, such as those used in the
Crunchy Carrot & Beet Salad (see page 53) or the Waldorf Salad
(see page 39). The mayo can be flavored with fresh herbs, mustard,
a touch of garlic, or whatever other flavors take your fancy.

1½ cups cashews
finely grated zest and juice of 1 lemon
1 scallion (white part only)
1 to 2 Medjool dates, pitted
2 teaspoons walnut oil or grapeseed oil
salt and pepper

Soak the cashews for about 8 hours, or overnight, until softened, to
make them easier to blend to a creamy consistency.
Drain and rinse the cashews then add to a high-speed blender with
the zest and juice of the lemon, the white part of the scallion, dates,
walnut or grapeseed oil, and 1 cup of water.
Blend on high speed until the dressing is smooth and similar in
consistency to heavy cream. Season to taste and add more water if
you prefer a thinner consistency.
Seal the mayo in a jar with a screw-top lid and place in the fridge
to chill until needed.

RED BELL PEPPER HUMMUS

This can be served as a raw dip or as a salad dressing. To use it as a
dressing, ensure the hummus has a pouring consistency by thinning
it with a little extra water. Team this with the Green-on-Green Salad
(see page 81) or Sweet Potato & Pea Salad (see page 73).

1 small zucchini, trimmed
2 large roasted red bell peppers
1½ cups sprouted chickpeas or any sprouted seeds
1 garlic clove, peeled
2 teaspoons sesame seeds
finely grated zest and juice of 1 large lemon
salt and pepper

Peel the zucchini and put it in a food processor with the rest of the
ingredients and ½ cup water. Blend until smooth, season, and thin
with a little extra water, if needed.

ASIAN-INSPIRED DRESSING

The miso paste enhances the richness of this sweet, sour, and
spicy dressing. It goes well with any vegetable "noodle" dish—try
it instead of the Coconut Curry Sauce on the Vegetable "Noodles"
(see page 93), with the Beet Carpaccio (see page 47), or the Mango,
Beet, Kale & Radish Salad (see page 109).

¼-inch piece fresh ginger root, peeled
1 garlic clove, peeled
2 tablespoons sesame oil
finely grated zest and juice of 1 lime
2 Medjool dates, pitted
2 tablespoons miso paste
2 tablespoons soy sauce

Grate the ginger and garlic. Blend all the ingredients together with
2 tablespoons water in a high-speed blender or food processor
until combined.

BASIC PESTO

Pesto is a staunch friend when it comes to dressings.
I like to thin it down with a little lemon juice, raw
apple cider vinegar, or other flavorsome liquid that
is compatible with dressings, for an instant sauce to
anoint a salad or steamed or roasted vegetables.

Pesto doesn't have to be the traditional basil, pine nut,
garlic, and Parmesan combination; you can use other
soft-leaf herbs or greens, such as spinach, nettle tops,
collard greens, or kale instead of the basil. Likewise,
pine nuts can be replaced with pistachios, Brazil nuts,
almonds, roasted peanuts, walnuts, or sunflower seeds.
Or, you can make a red pesto using tomatoes, roasted
bell peppers, and chiles. Ditch the cheese or use a
different vegan alternative. The options available are
almost endless.

3 tablespoons pine nuts, almonds,
pistachios, cashews, or pumpkin seeds,
or nut or seed of your choice
1 peeled garlic clove, or 1 peeled shallot,
or 1 trimmed scallion
1 small handful of basil leaves,
cilantro, mint, tarragon, parsley,
arugula, cavolo nero (dino kale), or herb
of your choice
2 tablespoons vegan hard cheese
1 teaspoon lemon juice
(to keep the pesto green)
¼ cup cold-pressed extra virgin olive oil,
plus extra to cover
salt

Blitz the nuts or seeds and garlic in a food processor.
Add the basil, or green leaves or herb of your choice,
the vegan hard cheese and pulse again.
Add the lemon juice and olive oil and pulse again
until combined to a coarse consistency similar to a
sauce. Season with salt to taste.
Spoon the pesto into an airtight jar with a lid, add enough
oil to cover, and store in the fridge for up to 1 week.

SPRING CABBAGE & KALE PESTO

This greens-based pesto works equally well without the vegan hard cheese. Substitute almonds, macadamia nuts, or hazelnuts for the peanuts, and use it to dress the Avocado "Truffle" Salad (see page 27), Summer Squash Salad (see page 37), or the Crunchy Winter Vegetable Salad (see page 75).

1 handful of spring cabbage or collard greens
1 small bunch of cavolo nero (dino kale)
3 garlic cloves, peeled
¼ cup grated vegan hard cheese
3 tablespoons cold-pressed extra virgin olive oil, plus extra to cover
¼ cup unsalted roasted peanuts
finely grated zest and juice of 1 lemon
salt and pepper

Tear or cut the leaves off of the tough stems of the spring cabbage and cavolo nero (dino kale). Blanch the greens in boiling salted water for about 1 minute until softened in texture and flavor, then drain well and pat dry with paper towels.

Coarsely chop the greens (you can juice the stems) and add to a food processor with the other ingredients then process until finely chopped to the consistency you desire. Season and process briefly again.

Spoon the pesto into an airtight jar with a screwtop lid, add enough oil to cover, and store in the fridge for up to 1 week.

LEMONY SALSA VERDE

Bright, fresh, and bracing, this dressing is great with the Radish, Beet & Orange Salad (see page 35) and the Avocado, Tomato & Lettuce Salad (see page 38), or served poured over grilled chicken or fish.

finely grated zest and juice of 1 lemon
1 shallot, peeled
1 garlic clove, peeled
1 handful of mixed herbs, such as parsley, chives, cilantro, mint, and dill
½ cup cold-pressed extra virgin olive oil
salt and pepper

Add the lemon zest and juice to a food processor with the shallot, garlic, and herbs. Process briefly until coarsely chopped, then gradually add the olive oil through the funnel, with the motor still running, until you have a fairly smooth dressing. Season to taste.

GREMOLATA-STYLE DRESSING

Gremolata is a popular Italian herb and lemon condiment, and in this recipe the essence of the accompaniment is turned into a fresh and zesty dressing that goes well with the Summer Squash Salad (see page 37).

finely grated zest and juice of 1 lemon and 1 lime
2 to 3 tablespoons cold-pressed extra virgin olive oil
1 handful of chopped mixed herbs, such as dill, mint, basil, and chives
1 to 2 teaspoons date paste or sweetener of choice
1 small green chile, seeded (optional)
salt and pepper

Blend together all the ingredients in a high-speed blender or food processor, or beat together by hand until smooth. Season to taste.

TOMATO DRESSING

Delicious with the Swiss Chard & Tomato Salad (see page 83), this dressing also works well as a raw pasta sauce with vegetable "noodles," as well as being a type of raw ketchup.

If you're keeping the dressing completely raw, use the date paste as a sweetener and omit the mustard.

2 cups cherry tomatoes
1 large red bell pepper
2 shallots, peeled
1 large garlic clove, peeled
1 handful of mixed herbs, such as basil, parsley, and oregano
1 teaspoon date paste or maple syrup
1 teaspoon wholegrain mustard
finely grated zest and juice of 1 lemon
salt and pepper

Seed and coarsely chop the tomatoes and pepper. Blitz all the dressing ingredients together in a food processor until liquefied, but still slightly chunky. Season to taste.

PEANUT SATAY DRESSING

Ready-made peanut butter provides a nifty shortcut to a quick dressing, but you can make your own by blending blanched or roasted peanuts with a tiny amount of oil in a blender. This dressing works well with the Carrot "Noodle" Salad (see page 89).

3 tablespoons organic peanut butter or tahini
3 tablespoons orange juice
salt and pepper

Beat together all the dressing ingredients with 1 tablespoon water in a bowl. Season to taste.

ZA'ATAR DRESSING

Za'atar is a Middle Eastern blend of thyme, oregano, sumac, and sesame seeds and gives a truly unique flavor to a salad dressing. Here, the spice and herb mixture is teamed up with chiles, lemon juice, and sesame oil to make a dressing that goes well with the Smashed Cucumber Salad (see page 74).

2 tablespoons sesame oil
2 teaspoons lemon juice
1 to 2 teaspoons za'atar
1 to 2 red chiles, seeded, depending on how hot the chiles are or how spicy you like your dressing
salt and pepper

To make the dressing, beat together the sesame oil, lemon juice, and za'atar. Finely chop the red chiles and stir them in. Season to taste.

MOROCCAN DRESSING

This aromatic dressing features the beautiful North African spice blend ras-el-hanout, which is usually made up of at least 20 different ingredients. The blend I use includes galangal, black pepper, ginger, cardamom, cayenne, allspice, nigella, cinnamon, cassia, coriander seeds, nutmeg, cloves, mace, lavender, and dried rose buds and has a wonderful fragrant, warming flavor. Serve the dressing with the Middle Eastern-inspired Summer Salad (see page 51).

1½ teaspoons ras-el-hanout, plus extra to serve
3 tablespoons walnut or pistachio oil
juice of 1 lemon
1 to 2 teaspoons date paste or sweetener of choice
1 small red chile, seeded (optional)
salt and pepper

Blend together all the ingredients in a high-speed blender or food processor, or beat them by hand. Slowly trickling the oil in with the machine running helps thicken and emulsify the dressing.

Season to taste, then seal in a jar with a screwtop lid and store in the fridge until needed (it will keep for up to 1 week). Serve garnished with a whole star anise, if you wish.

GINGER & WASABI DRESSING

This dressing lends a fiery kick to simple salads such as the Rainbow Chard & Black Radish Salad (see page 61).

1-inch piece fresh ginger root, peeled
1 tablespoon lime juice
2 tablespoons cold-pressed extra virgin olive oil
1 to 2 teaspoons wasabi paste

Grate the ginger and mix together with the rest of ingredients, adjusting the quantity of wasabi to taste.

CREAMY TURMERIC DRESSING

This creamy yellow dressing adds a bolt of color to a salad as well as providing anti-inflammatory and other amazing medicinal benefits, thanks to the fresh turmeric. It looks and tastes great with the Zucchini & Candy Cane Beet Salad (see page 69).

¾ cup cashews
1-inch piece fresh turmeric or 2 teaspoons ground turmeric
1 tablespoon raw apple cider vinegar
salt and pepper

Blend the cashews with the other dressing ingredients and ½ cup water in a high-speed blender until smooth and creamy. If your blender isn't powerful enough to bring everything to a smooth consistency, either juice the turmeric first (or use 2 teaspoons ground turmeric) and soak the cashew nuts for about 8 hours, or overnight, before blending.

ACAI BERRY DRESSING

The acai berry is a wonder food in terms of nutritional value and makes a great dressing with its naturally sweet-sour taste. It is often sold in powdered form so is easy to incorporate into smoothies and dressings, and its stunning dark purple color complements the Red Cabbage & Zucchini Ruffle Salad (see page 33) perfectly.

2 teaspoons acai berry powder
3 tablespoons apple juice
1 teaspoon pomegranate molasses

To make the dressing, blend the ingredients together until smooth.

SPIRULINA DRESSING

Spirulina is a type of blue-green algae superfood. I've used the powdered kind here. It is an acquired taste, so add more sweetener if the dressing is too bitter for you. I serve it with the Arugula & Radish Salad (see page 97) or drizzle a fresh fruit salad with it.

½ teaspoon spirulina powder
finely grated zest and juice of 1 lemon
2 teaspoons date paste or sweetener of choice

Blend together all the ingredients until smooth.

RAW "CHOCOLATE" SAUCE

Raw cacao is a delicious superfood, full of antioxidants, vitamins, and minerals. This recipe makes a rich, glossy sauce, which is a great alternative to the white chocolate sauce for the Snowberry Salad (see page 115). Or, simply pour it onto banana ice cream.

¼ cup coconut oil
1 vanilla bean
3 tablespoons raw cacao powder
2 tablespoons sweetener of choice

Gently melt the coconut oil and scrape the seeds from the vanilla bean. Place all the ingredients in a high-speed blender and process to a silky, dark-colored chocolate sauce.

SPICED YOGURT DRIZZLE

Yogurt makes a wonderful dip, drizzle, or dressing for any sweet or savory dish, but if you're dairy-free then try a nut-based or coconut yogurt alternative. Serve this spiced yogurt with chopped fresh fruit, as a dip for sweet crudités, or poured onto the Red Fruit Salad (see page 111) or Dragon Fruit Salad (see page 99), with or without the passion fruit and clementine dressing.

1 cup raw yogurt (made with
¾ cup cashews, ½ cup coconut water, and 2 pitted Medjool dates blended until smooth)
finely grated zest and juice of 1 orange
2 teaspoons maple syrup or sweetener of choice
½ teaspoon berbere spice mix, sumac, or ground cinnamon

Beat or blend together all the ingredients until combined. Serve scattered with orange zest and sprinkled with sumac and garnished with a cinnamon stick, if you wish.

Left-right: Creamy Turmeric Dressing, Spiced Yogurt Drizzle, Spirulina Dressing, Za'atar Dressing, Moroccan Dressing.

toppings

There are almost endless esthetic, flavorsome, and nutritious things you can scatter or sprinkle your salad with to add a final flourish, a bit of pizzazz, a flavor explosion, and hopefully the "wow" factor that will get people coming back for second helpings.

Why add toppings and sprinkles

✳ to add variety and excitement to your salads.

✳ to provide a final layer of flavor and color.

✳ to add a protein element, including nuts and seeds, or tofu.

✳ to add an extra textural element—placed on top, rather than mixed in, your topping will stay crisp and crunchy for longer.

CUSTOMIZE YOUR SALAD!

I always love to add a few finishing touches to my salads. It can be as simple as a handful of fresh-from-the-garden herbs or sparkling, jewel-like pomegranate seeds to more elaborate flavor-packed vegetable powders, or a palate-teasing umami sprinkle. All of these, and my ideas below, will add another element of visual interest, flavor, and texture to your salads.

The following are just some of my favorite things I use to customize salads (bear in mind that toppings or sprinkles are best added at the last minute, so they don't get soggy or even lost in the salad):

✳ Edible fresh flowers, including floral, herb, and vegetable flowers. Szechuan buttons (little yellow flowerbuds) are worth hunting down and give a tingling sensation when you eat them.

✳ Baby salad leaves, pea shoots, microgreens, microherbs, or pale green celery leaves.

✳ Baby vegetables, including carrots or zucchini, or vegetable or herb seedlings, or thinly shaved vegetables slices.

✳ Microplane-grated nuts, such as almonds and macadamia nuts, for a Parmesan-like topping.

✳ Nuts and seeds (whole or chopped), plain, toasted, or sweet-spiced, or savory granola.

✳ Attractively or artfully cut fruits and vegetables.

✳ Wild and foraged blackberries, elderflowers, ramson leaves or flowers, or dandelion leaves.

✳ Fronds of decorative herbs, such as dill or bronze fennel.

✳ Colorful dried fruit.

✳ Croutons (toasted, baked, or fried) made from sourdough, rye, polenta, potatoes, or sweet potatoes.

✳ Colorful fruit, vegetable, and superfood powders, including blueberry, citrus, tomato, herb, acai berry, spirulina, or chlorella.

✳ Seaweed, or other edible sea vegetables, such as nori sheets, kombu, or seaweed "confetti".

✳ Sprouted seeds and beans.

✳ Cooked vegetables, such as caramelized roasted vegetables.

✳ Pickles and fermented vegetables, such as olives, capers, caperberries, or kimchi.

✳ Coconut shavings, chai seeds, or toasted buckwheat.

✳ Vegetable "chips," dehydrated fruits and vegetables, or crispy fried herbs.

✳ Edible glitter or edible gold leaf or powder for special occasions.

SPICED POTATO CROUTONS

You can make these with sweet potatoes or white potatoes, but the latter will take slightly longer to cook.

4 to 5 large potatoes, scrubbed
3 tablespoons cold-pressed extra virgin olive oil or melted coconut oil
2 teaspoons dried or chopped fresh herbs
1 teaspoon ras-el-hanout
2 garlic cloves, peeled and finely chopped
salt and pepper

Preheat the oven to 425°F and warm 2 to 3 roasting pans.

Cut the potatoes into ¼-inch dice and put them in a bowl with the oil, herbs, spice, garlic, and some seasoning then turn until evenly coated. Tip them onto the warmed roasting pans and spread out into a single, even layer.

Roast the potatoes for 20 to 30 minutes or until cooked through, golden brown, and crisp. Transfer to a dish lined with paper towels until ready to serve.

RAW "PARMESAN"

A dairy-free alternative for a "sprinkling" cheese. It has the fine graininess of grated Parmesan and a similar salty, savory flavor.

1 cup walnuts or ¾ cup blanched almonds
1 small garlic clove, peeled
½ teaspoon sea salt flakes

Add to a food processor and blitz to a fine grainy consistency.

FRIED SAGE LEAVES

Often served as part of an apéritif in Italy, these also make a great crisp topping for a salad—even if you're not a big lover of sage, the leaves seem to mellow in flavor when cooked this way.

2 tablespoons sunflower oil
1 handful of sage leaves
½ teaspoon sea salt flakes

Warm the oil in a shallow skillet over medium heat and fry the sage leaves until bright green and crisp.

Remove, drain on paper towels, and sprinkle with salt before serving.

MARINATED MUSHROOMS

The flavor of the mushrooms improves the longer they marinate.

1lb mushrooms (white are fine but other varieties such as shitake, shimeji, enoki, crimini, and oyster mushrooms are more flavorful), trimmed
¼ cup cold-pressed extra virgin olive oil
2 tablespoons white wine vinegar
2 to 3 garlic cloves, peeled and thinly sliced
juice of 1 lemon
a pinch of sugar (optional)
1 small handful of mixed herbs, such as tarragon, oregano, parsley, and thyme
salt and pepper

Tear the mushrooms into pieces, or cut any extra-large ones into bite-sized chunks, and set aside.

In a large bowl, beat all the remaining ingredients together and add the mushrooms. Season, stir the mushrooms to coat, then cover and let marinate for 20 minutes or, better still, place in the fridge overnight.

Serve the mushrooms at room temperature.

CHINESE SEAWEED KALE

Essentially the same as kale chips, but by finely shredding the kale it becomes just like the crispy seaweed you get in Chinese restaurants.

1 large bunch of kale
2 teaspoons cold-pressed extra virgin olive oil
½ teaspoon sea salt flakes

Preheat the oven to 300°F and line 2 baking pans with nonstick parchment paper.

Tear the kale leaves off of the tough stems (you can juice the stems). Finely chop the leaves and toss them in the olive oil and salt until evenly coated.

Spread the kale out on the lined baking pans and cook in the oven for 5 to 10 minutes, turning once, until deep green in color and crisp. Remove from the oven and let cool.

COCONUT "BACON"

A nifty vegan way to replicate the savoriness of traditional bacon.

2 tablespoons liquid smoke (or use 1 tablespoon
smoked paprika mixed with 1 teaspoon water)
2 tablespoons soy sauce, tamari, or nama shoyu
1 tablespoon maple syrup or sweetener of choice
2 cups coconut flakes (the larger the
flakes the better)

Preheat the oven to 350°F and line 2 large baking pans with nonstick parchment paper.

In a medium-sized bowl, whisk together all the ingredients, except the coconut flakes, with 1 tablespoon water. Once combined, gently stir the coconut flakes into the liquid and stir gently to coat.

Remove the coconut flakes using a slotted spoon and spread them out in an even layer on the lined baking pans. Bake for 2 to 5 minutes until crisp and browned, then transfer to a wire rack to cool. The coconut "bacon" will keep stored in an airtight container for up to 1 week.

DRIED APPLE RINGS

Dehydration is a useful method for preserving fruits (and vegetables) and they make a nutritious addition to a salad.

4 to 5 eating apples, peeled if the skin is tough
2 tablespoons lemon juice

Preheat the oven to 150°F.

Core and slice the apples into rings $1/8$ inch in thickness and brush with the lemon juice to stop them from discoloring. Place directly onto the racks in the oven, making sure the rings are spaced out, and cook for 6 to 12 hours until dry but still slightly pliable. Let cool. This works for most fruits, including mango, strawberries, and kiwi.

SUPER SEED & NUT SPRINKLE

This nutrient-rich blend of ground nuts and seeds is great to sprinkle over anything you fancy, not just salads.

2 to 3 tablespoons each of walnuts, almonds,
pumpkin seeds, sunflower seeds, sesame seeds,
hemp seeds, and chia seeds

Add the nuts and seeds to a food processor fitted with an "S" blade and blitz to a coarse, grainy consistency. Alternatively, use a coffee grinder to make a finer mixture. Store in an airtight container.

UMAMI SPRINKLE

In Japan, umami is classed as the fifth sense of taste. It adds an amazing depth of flavor to savory dishes. There are lots of ready-made versions available, but it's easy to make your own. Sprinkle directly onto your salads just before serving.

1oz dried shitake or dried porcini mushrooms
1 tablespoon ready-made tomato powder, or make
your own (see page 140)
1 tablespoon kelp powder or kombu
1 teaspoon sea salt flakes
a pinch of garlic salt
a pinch of dried oregano
a pinch of dried red chile flakes
a few grinds of black pepper

Place all the ingredients in a food processor, blender, or coffee grinder and blitz to a fine powder. Store in an airtight container for up to 2 to 3 months.

NUT & SEED "BRITTLE"

Scattering savory as well as sweet salads with this "brittle" adds flavor and crunch.

$\frac{3}{4}$ cup pumpkin seeds
3 tablespoons sesame seeds
1 cup chopped hazelnuts
$\frac{1}{2}$ cup raw buckwheat
2 tablespoons sweetener of choice
a pinch of dried red chile flakes

Preheat the oven to 300°F and line a baking pan with nonstick parchment paper.

Mix together all the ingredients in a bowl with 1 tablespoon water. Spread out the mixture in an even layer on the lined baking pan. Bake for 20 to 30 minutes or until golden and crisp, then let cool before breaking into pieces.

For a more savory version, add a small handful of nori flakes or shredded nori sheets.

For a sweeter version, combine the nuts and seeds with ¼ cup dried fruit, such as golden raisins, cranberries, or cherries, 1 tablespoon maple syrup or sweetener of choice, and 1 tablespoon melted coconut oil.

Left-right: dehydrated fruit; hemp seeds; bread croutons; kale "chips"; Coconut "Bacon"; dried chile flakes

QUICK PICKLED VEGETABLES

It's quick and easy to pickle vegetables. They add great flavor and crunch to salads.

2 tablespoons mirin or rice wine vinegar
3 tablespoons lime juice
3 tablespoons vegan fish sauce
1 tablespoon granulated sugar
1 garlic clove, peeled and grated
2 teaspoons grated fresh ginger root
10½oz prepared and very finely sliced or grated crunchy vegetables, such as radishes, celery, fennel, mooli, carrots, cabbages, or cucumber
pepper

To make the pickling liquor, beat together the mirin or rice vinegar, lime juice, fish sauce, sugar, garlic, and ginger root in a large bowl until the sugar dissolves. Season with pepper.

Add the vegetables to the pickling liquor, stir to combine, and let marinate for 10 to 30 minutes at room temperature.

Just before serving, lift the vegetables out of the pickling liquor and use as you desire. (The pickling liquor can be added to a dressing.)

QUICK PICKLED SHALLOTS

If you dislike the acidity of raw shallots or onions in a salad then giving them a quick bath in a sweet vinegar marinade draws out any bitterness and leaves them with a milder oniony flavor.

2 tablespoons red wine vinegar
3 tablespoons cold-pressed extra virgin olive oil
1 teaspoon granulated sugar
1 large shallot or similar-sized onion, peeled and thinly sliced
1 garlic clove, peeled and thinly sliced
salt and pepper

To make the pickling liquor, beat together the vinegar, olive oil, and sugar in a bowl until the sugar dissolves.

Add the shallot and garlic to the pickling liquor, stir to combine, and let marinate for 30 minutes at room temperature.

Just before serving, lift out the shallot and garlic and use as you desire. (Save the pickling liquor to use for a dressing.)

QUICK PICKLED FRUIT

Fresh fruit can taste just as good pickled as vegetables do. You can leave the skin on the apples, peaches, and nectarines because they soften during the pickling process.

2 tablespoons red or white wine vinegar
1 teaspoon granulated sugar
2 handfuls of prepared and sliced fruit, such as peaches, apples, watermelon, nectarines, or pineapple
1 shallot
salt and pepper

To make the pickling liquor, beat together the vinegar, sugar, and seasoning in a bowl until the sugar dissolves.

Add the fruit and shallot to the pickling liquor, stir to combine, and let marinate for 20 to 30 minutes at room temperature.

Just before serving, lift out the fruit and shallot and use as you desire. (The pickling liquor can be added to a dressing.)

PICKLED SPICED GRAPES

Grapes give little bursts of sweetness to a salad. These quick-pickled ones are also gently spiced with a slight acidic kick from the vinegar, and add a completely different flavor dimension to a salad.

1½ cups rice wine vinegar
2 tablespoons granulated sugar
2 star anise
½ teaspoon fennel seeds
1 to 2 teaspoons dried red chile flakes
1 teaspoon salt
3 tablespoons orange juice
2 handfuls of small seedless grapes

To make the pickling liquor, beat together the vinegar, sugar, star anise, fennel seeds, red chile flakes, salt, orange juice, and $1/3$ cup water in a bowl until the sugar dissolves.

Pick the grapes from their stalks. Add them to the pickling liquid, stir to combine, and let marinate at room temperature for 30 minutes, or in the fridge overnight.

Remove the grapes from the pickling liquid (you can keep the liquid to use in a dressing). The pickled grapes can be made a few days ahead of serving and stored in the fridge.

FRUIT, VEGETABLE & HERB POWDERS

These powders are easy to make and give salads a fantastic flavor boost when sprinkled on as a finishing touch. Use sparingly because the flavor is highly concentrated.

Drying the prepared ingredients in a dehydrator is ideal but spreading them out on a wire rack or on a baking pan set in an oven preheated to 150°F, or as low as your oven will go, works well too.

Grind dry and brittle ingredients in batches. The best tools for grinding are a spice mill, coffee mill, or a high-speed blender.

Use the powders immediately or store for up to 6 months in an airtight jar to keep them completely dry.

Don't reserve the powders just for salads because you can also use them for smoothies, granola, soups, sauces, desserts, and baked goods, such as cakes, cookies, and bread doughs.

Here are five to try, but do experiment with other flavors:

BEET POWDER

Very finely slice 4 to 6 raw scrubbed or peeled beets.
Place in the oven for 3 to 4 hours, or until completely dry and brittle and then grind.

HERB POWDER

Spread out 2 bunches of soft-leaf herbs, such as parsley, cilantro, thyme, sage, and dill, on a wire rack or baking pan. Place in the oven for 90 minutes, or until completely dry and brittle and then grind.

FRUIT & VEGETABLE POWDER

Prepare fruit and vegetables, such as strawberries, raspberries, kiwi, citrus, rhubarb, apples or carrots, by removing any tough skin as necesary. Cut into thin slices, bearing in mind that wet ingredients will take longer to dry out. Place in the oven for 5 to 6 hours, or until completely dry and brittle and then grind.

TOMATO POWDER

Slice 1lb 2 oz tomatoes as thinly as you possibly can.
Place in the oven for 5 to 6 hours, turning once, or until completely dry and brittle and then grind.

CITRUS PEEL POWDER

Cut the peel from 4 to 5 citrus fruits such as oranges, lemons, and grapefruit. Place the peel in a saucepan, add enough cold water to cover then bring to a boil and cook for 1 minute. Drain, rinse well in cold water, drain again, then pat dry.
Place in the oven for 18 to 24 hours until completely dry and brittle and then grind.

INDEX

ABOUT AMBER

Amber's love of fruit and vegetables started from a young age. Her parents had a large vegetable garden, so there was always a bountiful supply of fresh fruit, vegetables, salad crops, and herbs right on the doorstep.

She previously worked in corporate marketing, and also ran her own freelance marketing consultancy. She discovered the concept of the raw food diet two years ago, and decided to try it out as an experiment. She was so blown away by how amazing it made her feel that after just a few days she carried on eating that way.

Amber now eats an 80 to 90 percent raw diet for health and vitality. She still happily cooks other foods for the rest of her family but just tries to find enticing and inventive ways to encourage them to include more (raw) fruit and vegetables in their diets.

One of Amber's passions is making salads. She also composes artful arrangements of fruit and vegetables, turning them into eye-catching patterns and designs, which she sells as limited edition prints.

ACKNOWLEDGMENTS

Thanks firstly to my parents for all their love and amazing support. For growing things, sourcing, measuring up, painting background boards, dog-sitting when I'm busy etc., etc. The list is endless! I couldn't do any of this without you. Also for passing on your passions (and a little of your creative talents!) for food, cooking, and art.

To my partner Mark and our beloved chocolate Labrador Max; your encouragement (and woofing!) spurs me on every day.

To "Juice Queen" Kara Rosen who spotted me on Instagram and gave me my first commission—I will be forever grateful. To Calgary Avansino and Valentina Zelyaeva for introducing me to the concept of raw food and sparking a fascination that quite literally changed my life.

To Viv Irish and Joy Hales (editors at *Derbyshire Life* magazine) who gave me my first break in food writing. To Jamie O and Pete, big thanks for your interest in what I do and for introducing me to the wonderful world of Instagram and the candy cane beets!

To the fabulous team at Octopus: to Stephanie Jackson for your gorgeous joie de vivre, enthusiasm, and faith in me; to Yasia Williams for your creative genius and sweet patience with my endless flow of photographs; to Polly Poulter for editing me so beautifully, and to Karen Baker and the PR team for all their energies and activities in promoting this book. Also to my lovely literary agent Jo Cavey for appearing in my life at just the right moment.

Finally to my "family" on social media, Instagram, and to all those who follow my work—without you this book wouldn't be here.